Richmond Castle and Easby Abbey

John Goodall

CONTENTS

Tour of Richmond 3
Overview and Setting 3
Castle Enclosure 4
Robin Hood Tower 6
Hall and Adjoining Ranges 7
South Curtain Wall 13
West Curtain Wall 13
Keep, or Great Tower 14
Cells 17

History of Richmond 19

Special Features
Castle and Town 5
Alan Rufus, 'the Red' 10
Cockpit Garden 12
Honour of Richmond 22
Audit Money 29
Cell Block and the
 'Richmond Sixteen' 30

Tour of Easby 33
Overview and Setting 35
Gatehouse 36
West Range 37
Refectory 38
Cloister and
 Chapter House 41
Church 42
Northern Buildings 43

History of Easby 45

Special Features
The Premonstratensians 39
Parish Church of St Agatha
 of Easby 40
Furnishings of the Abbey 46
Visitations to the Abbey 51

Plans
Richmond   inside back cover
Easby 34

TOUR OF RICHMOND: OVERVIEW AND SETTING

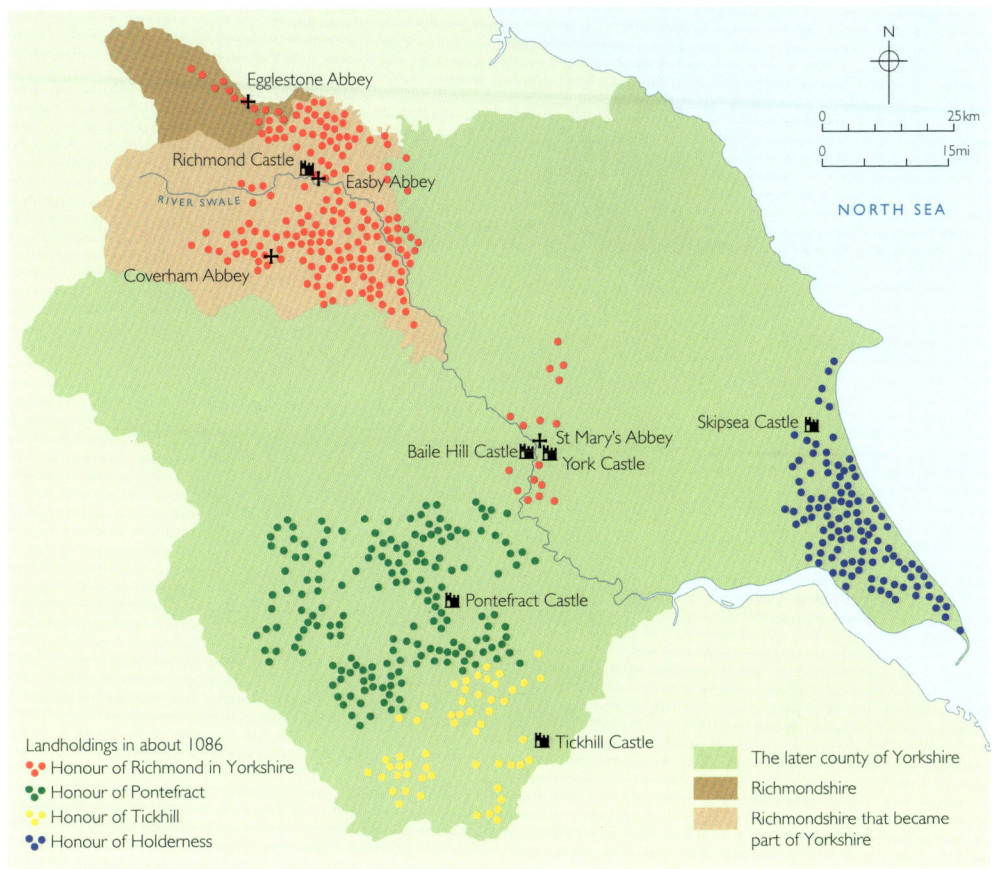

Tour of Richmond

OVERVIEW AND SETTING

Richmond was one in a group of four major castles – with Tickhill, Pontefract and Skipsea – that staked out the Norman Conquest of Yorkshire in the 1070s. It was laid out on a virgin hill-top site commanding a crossing of the river Swale. Roughly equidistant from it are two important earlier centres: Catrice (Catterick), two miles south, which had been a Roman fort on the road called Dere Street (in this area roughly on the line of the A1); and Ghellinges (Gilling West), two miles north. At the time of the Conquest both Catterick and Gilling West were seats of the powerful Anglo-Saxon Edwin (d.1071), Earl of Mercia, but were granted to Alan Rufus at Edwin's defeat.

Richmond Castle was probably intended to help define and reinforce England's northern border with Scotland. The estate, or Honour, attached to the castle was vast, with lands across eight counties supporting 180 knights. Its heartland comprised one consolidated landholding, which came to form a distinct administrative and ecclesiastical unit known from the late 12th century as Richmondshire. It developed its own network of religious foundations and subsidiary castles patronized or built by the knightly families supported by the Honour.

Above: Map showing the four major honours – castles and their associated landholdings – that staked out the Norman Conquest in Yorkshire

Facing page: The 11th-century north entrance to Richmond Castle

TOUR OF RICHMOND: CASTLE ENCLOSURE

Above: The castle is cut from the roughly circular hill-top settlement of Richmond like a slice in a cake

Below right: The original, 11th-century, north entrance to the castle, preserved in the base of the keep

Below: The 12th-century north castle entrance beside the keep, seen in ruins in this engraving of 1786. Blocked up at the base of the keep is the 11th-century entrance and, to the bottom right, beside Robin Hood Tower, the now vanished postern gate that ran below the wall level

CASTLE ENCLOSURE

The castle buildings stand within a roughly triangular enclosure. At its apex, to the north, is the keep, or great tower. The enclosure was protected towards the town on two sides by ditches and a massively thick curtain wall, and to the south by the cliffs dropping to the Swale. It is entered today through a large gateway beside the keep; in the 11th century this north entrance was a little to the west, through a gateway that survives fossilized in the base of the keep. When the keep was built in the 12th century the north entrance was moved to its current position. It was rebuilt as it appears today in the 1850s. Three other gateways existed in the 11th century: one in the

TOUR OF RICHMOND: CASTLE AND TOWN

south-east corner of the enclosure, which remains, and two smaller postern gates. One of these also survives, in the south-west corner. The other was immediately to the north of Robin Hood Tower in the east curtain wall (see page 6).

Probably at the same time as the building of the keep a small fortified courtyard, known as a barbican, was built fronting the market place to protect the north entrance. Its form is retained in the semicircle of walls and buildings around the base of the keep. It once had a gatehouse, recorded in a survey of 1538 (see page 26), which notes an 'outer gatehouse called the porter's lodge' at the entrance to the barbican. This was approached across a drawbridge.

Along the east curtain wall were three square-planned towers, one of which has collapsed. Several doors and openings survive in this stretch of the wall, evidence of buildings that would have lined it. Above the cliffs to the south are the remains of Scolland's Hall, the principal domestic building of the castle enclosure.

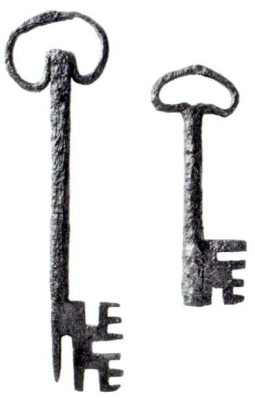

Above: Two medieval iron door keys found at Richmond Castle

Castle and Town

The castle and its settlement were laid out as one to a roughly circular plan on a virgin hill-top site. A wall surrounded the whole and at the centre was the large market place – a reminder that the function of Norman castles was as much economic as military. To the south, cut from the whole like a slice of cake, was the castle enclosure. The rest of the settlement comprised radiating plots (burgages) for houses and gardens, probably for those serving castle guard and for other townspeople.

To the east of the castle enclosure is the Cockpit (see page 12), once thought to date from the 12th century, but now believed to be an original 11th-century feature. In the mid 12th century the keep was built, dominating the town and market. In about 1540 the antiquarian John Leland described the area around the market as 'The Bailey', suggesting that the town was once deemed part of the castle. He noted, too, that the town was walled and its streets paved, although the walls were in ruins, as were the three principal town gates. The form of this larger settlement remains clearly legible in the layout of the town today.

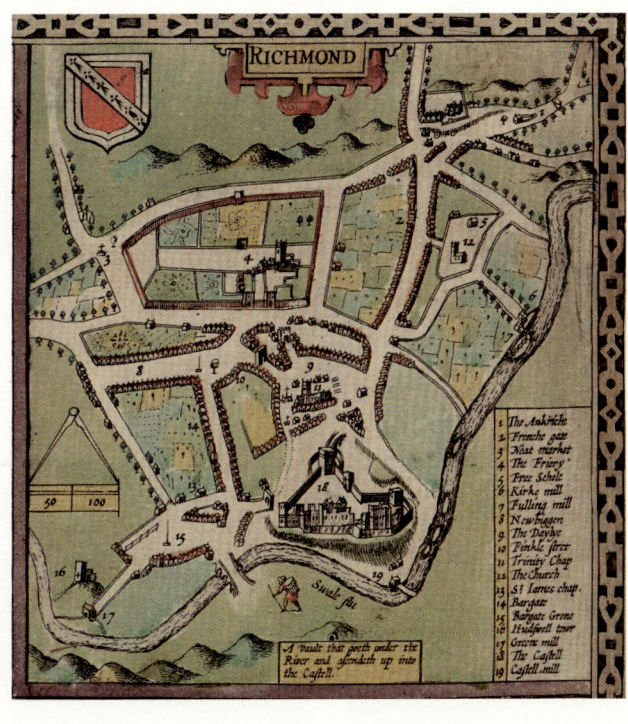

Below: A map of about 1611, drawn by John Speed, showing the town and castle of Richmond. The castle barbican and its drawbridge can be seen to the north of the keep

TOUR OF RICHMOND: ROBIN HOOD TOWER

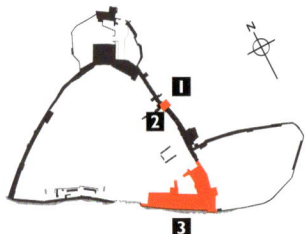

◼ ROBIN HOOD TOWER

The first tower along the east curtain wall is known as Robin Hood Tower (a name probably born of Victorian romanticism). As first built, between 1071 and 1093, the tower rose only to the wall walk, with two barrel-vaulted chambers, set one above the other. The ground-floor chamber was a chapel (see below). The first-floor chamber was restored in 1836 and 1910–11; its use is unknown. It was entered from a short passage within the depth of the curtain wall above the original postern gate (now vanished); such wall, or mural, passages are a distinctive feature of grand Romanesque architecture, and are seen in other 11th-century English castle wall towers, such as those at Ludlow in Shropshire.

In about 1300 a second floor was added at wall-walk level. It served as a lodging chamber; its fireplace and a narrow window survive. At the same time a walkway was jettied out behind the tower to allow people to pass along the wall walk around the tower without having to go down to ground level. The stone brackets that supported the walkway are still visible.

In the grass beside the tower are a medieval well and the footings of a medieval building.

◼ St Nicholas's Chapel

This chapel is a rare example of an 11th-century interior. It was dedicated to St Nicholas. Around the three inner walls of the chapel runs a stone bench and above it a series of arches that was once supported on columns. In this arrangement, quite common in castle design, each arch would have formed the canopy of a seat. A guide to the castle of 1821 noted that these seats were still 'divided by pilasters, and formerly ornamented

Above: A medieval lead bucket and iron handle found in the well that survives beside Robin Hood Tower
Below: The south wall of the chapel, with its stone bench beneath arches. Remains of painted decoration, and the columns that once supported these arches, were still visible in 1821
Right: Robin Hood Tower
A Remains of the arch of the east curtain postern gate
B Upper chamber fireplace
C Doorway to the first floor set within the thickness of the wall above the entrance arch
D Wall passage doorway
E Medieval well

TOUR OF RICHMOND: HALL AND ADJOINING RANGES

on the sides with sketches of figures drawn with red paint, some of the colours appearing yet very fresh'.

Opposite the small, central entrance is a window flanked by roundels. The altar stone, on which Mass was celebrated, filled the sill. A groove inside the window frame may have held a panel of stained glass and the rectangular recess allowed the whole to be closed by a shutter. To either side of the window arch are small niches, perhaps intended for candles or lights. A similar arrangement can be seen in an 11th-century altar niche at Hastings Castle in Sussex. In the window overarch are traces of crude red lines on a white background, perhaps the remains of underpainting that guided the artist in the final decorative scheme; it could date from the building of the chapel. The altar window is framed on the outside by a projecting panel of stone, a device used to highlight the position of the chapel.

³ HALL AND ADJOINING RANGES

The principal domestic apartments of the castle stood in the south-east corner of the enclosure. Within the ruins are the remains of a large 11th-century range, one of the very few grand castle buildings in England confidently dated to William the Conqueror's reign (1066–87). The main interior of this outstandingly important survival is the great hall, known as Scolland's Hall, but it also comprised, at its east end, a small chamber, a latrine tower (Gold Hole Tower) and a gate to the Cockpit. On the outer-facing walls to the south and to the east were wooden hoardings, creating a continuation of the wall walk of the south curtain wall and around the Cockpit garden; the fixing sockets for these hoardings survive.

Two further ranges were later added to the original hall range: one to the west in the 12th century and one along the east curtain wall in about 1300. This latter addition, as well as extensions to the east end of Scolland's Hall and its wall tower, may have been prompted by a fire: some of the masonry in the basement is pink, a sign of exposure to intense heat.

Above: Fragment of painted window glass depicting the Virgin mourning Christ, from between 1475 and 1525, found at the castle. The central window of St Nicholas's Chapel may once have contained such glass

Above left: One of the most important survivals at the castle is the well-preserved 11th-century interior of St Nicholas's Chapel, with its central window above the altar stone, flanked by roundels

Below: A Cistercian-ware ceramic cup decorated with white pipeclay, found in the well at Richmond Castle. Such cups were typical tableware of the late 15th century

TOUR OF RICHMOND: SCOLLAND'S HALL

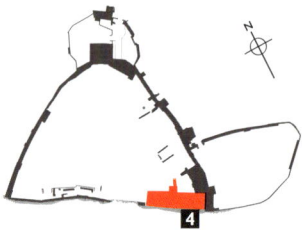

Below: *A roof support in the form of a carved head in the south-west corner of Scolland's Hall chamber*
Bottom: *Reconstruction drawing of Scolland's Hall as first built, c.1071–93*

4 Scolland's Hall

Scolland's Hall has been so known since at least 1400, and probably since the time of Scolland himself, the castle steward after whom it was named. He died between 1146 and 1150 and was a witness on charters for over 50 years – implying an unusually long life. The hall was the special charge of the steward: the place where the lord of the castle entertained and fed his household. It was on the first floor above an undercroft, a common arrangement in Norman and Anglo-Norman architecture. The sockets for its floor timbers are clearly visible. The entrance was in the north wall at the west end. Footings for the external stair that rose to this entrance are visible in the grass. The importance of the doorway is marked by flanking columns. Beneath the spring of the arch above the left column is a ruggedly carved Corinthian capital, a reminder that the design of this building is informed by Roman architecture.

Along both sides of the hall was a series of windows. Those of the 11th century, most of which remain, each comprised two lights, without permanent glazing, divided by a central column. The shallow recess around each may have held shutters or wooden-framed panels of glass or vellum, greased to render it translucent. During the works of about 1300 the windows at the east end were altered: that to the north made into a door

TOUR OF RICHMOND: SCOLLAND'S HALL

to the new chapel and chamber range, and that to the south greatly enlarged to light the 'high' end of the hall, where the table for the lord and his most important guests stood.

The interior opened to a high-pitched roof. Running along either side, below the roof, was a decorative cornice of arches, some of which survives. It may be 11th century and, if so, may derive from similar, but external, cornices known, for example, in the 11th-century monastery of Jumièges in Normandy. Food must originally have been prepared in a free-standing kitchen and brought into the hall through the main door.

If the arrangements in the 11th century were the same as those after 1100, the main door was at the 'low' (west) end of the hall and the high table at the opposite (east) end. In the 12th century a range was added to the west, abutting this 'low' end. Three doors were punched through the wall, the central one through a former window. These gave access to a kitchen, buttery and pantry. A wooden screen may have concealed them from the rest of the hall. Two of these doors were later blocked. In the north corner of the west wall is another door that served a spiral stair leading to the roof and battlements.

Above: The 11th-century Scolland's Hall. The kitchen range (right) and chapel and chamber range (left) were added over the next two centuries
Below: A tiny, finely decorated medieval bronze and gilt ornamental purse found at Richmond, possibly worn on a charm bracelet
Bottom: A lord and his household dining in much the same style that the lords of Richmond would have done in Scolland's Hall (from a 15th-century French manuscript)

TOUR OF RICHMOND: ALAN RUFUS, 'THE RED'

Alan Rufus, 'the Red'

By 1086 Alan was one of the richest and most powerful men in England.

Above: *Alan Rufus, beneath the arms of Richmond (blue and gold check with a red border), flanked by his vassal knights; from the Register of the Honour of Richmond, c.1400*

Below: *A medieval metal mould, found at Richmond, used to cast strap or belt ends. In the image above, Alan and his knights wear belts over their surcoats*

'Earl Alan of Brittany struck well with his company. He struck like a baron. Right well the Bretons did. With the king he came to this land to help him in his war. He was his cousin, of his lineage, a nobleman of high descent. Much he served and loved the king. And he right well rewarded him. Richmond he gave him in the north, a good castle fair and strong.'
Anglo-Norman poet Geffrei Gaimar (fl.1136–7)

Alan Rufus (d.1093), founder of Richmond, was the second son of Count Eudo of Penthièvre, Regent of Brittany. Alan was in the service of William the Conqueror, his father's cousin, with whom he fought in the Hastings campaign of 1066.

For his service and loyalty he was richly rewarded with extensive estates in Norfolk, Suffolk and Cambridgeshire and, after 1071, with vast holdings in Yorkshire, the future Honour of Richmond (see pages 22–3).

He remained intensely loyal to William and to William's son and successor, William II. By 1086 he was one of the richest and most powerful men in England and had settled 40 followers, all but two of them Bretons, on his English lands.

Whether Alan married or not is unknown, but both he and, after his death, his brother and heir, Alan Niger, 'the Black', had an affair with Gunnhild, daughter of the former Anglo-Saxon king Harold II. She is recorded at the time as a nun at Wilton Abbey, so whether she legally married either of the brothers is unclear. Alan Rufus founded the great Benedictine abbey of St Mary at York and his body, having been interred at Bury St Edmunds, was eventually moved there at the request of the monks.

TOUR OF RICHMOND: GATEWAY TO THE COCKPIT

5 Scolland's Hall Chamber

At the east, or 'high', end of the hall is a door to a chamber overlooking the Cockpit entrance to the castle. This room was comfortably appointed with a fireplace and window in the east wall and a large window overlooking the view to the south. It was served by the latrine tower to the north (Gold Hole Tower). The door in the south-east corner gave access to a wooden gallery (now gone) overlooking the Cockpit garden.

The chamber was probably used by privileged guests as a withdrawing space. It had a pitched roof countersunk below the outer wall, which continued the line of the east curtain. The roofline remains in the masonry on the south wall. A carved head in the south-west corner (see page 8) would have supported a roof timber. During the works of about 1300 (see page 13) the window in the south wall was altered.

6 Gold Hole Tower

Projecting north from the hall chamber is Gold Hole Tower (so named from at least the 19th century, after a story of treasure found in a recess). The first floor, accessed from the hall chamber, contained latrines supported on an internal arch, the springs of which remain. They presumably drained into the outer ditch through an opening at the foot of the tower. A second floor was added during the works of about 1300. This upper room, with its own fireplace, formed a lodging at the level of the wall walk, from which it was accessed. Its door with a shouldered arch remains high on the west face of the tower.

7 Gateway to the Cockpit

In the undercroft of Scolland's Hall is a gateway to the Cockpit. It lacks any sculpted decoration, evidence that it was regarded as a subsidiary entrance to the castle. Above the gateway was a timber gallery off the hall chamber; its sockets survive in the wall. Sockets for a second, lower, gallery run the length of the outer wall of the hall, overlooking the cliff.

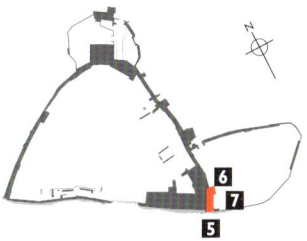

Below left: The Cockpit from the east. Above the gateway to Scolland's Hall is the doorway that led onto a gallery overlooking the garden. One of the latrine chutes of Gold Hole Tower is visible on the north face of the tower
Below: A ceramic urinal found at Richmond, dating from 1450 to 1550. Despite the latrines provided in Gold Hole Tower and elsewhere, urinals and chamber pots would have been in common use in private chambers
Bottom: The gateway from the undercroft of Scolland's Hall to the Cockpit. To its right is a door to a small chamber with a single window

11

TOUR OF RICHMOND: COCKPIT GARDEN

Cockpit Garden

A royal survey of 1280 documents a garden 'pertaining to the castle' – a probable reference to this area.

Above: *'The South east side of Richmond Castle with part of the Toune in 1674', by Francis Place. By this time the Cockpit was probably already in use for cockfighting, as well as a garden*

Below: *A gardener in an orchard in about 1470; detail from a Netherlandish manuscript. The view of Richmond of about 1400 appears to depict fruit trees in the Cockpit*

The name 'Cockpit' for this area probably followed its use for cockfighting, a widely popular sport from the 16th to the 18th centuries, and appears in a notebook of the 2nd Duke of Richmond, dated 1745. The original function of this area is not known, but it was from the start integral to the overall plan of the castle (see page 5). Its first defences were probably earth and timber; the style of the present stone defences suggests they were built in the mid 12th century, at about the same time as the keep.

A gateway, also of the 12th century, in the north wall of these defences, faces back along the line of the castle wall towards the town. There are good views of the wall towers through the gateway arch and also of the former outer ditch.

A view of the castle dating to about 1400 (see page 23) shows the Cockpit filled with what appear to be fruit trees. This, and the reference to a garden in the 1280 survey, suggest it may have been a garden from the foundation of the castle. If so, the timber hoarding off the chamber over the gateway may well have been built as much for the delightful views as for defence.

Excavation of the Cockpit has revealed evidence of 19th-century gardens, including the remains of ornamental flower beds, paths and a glasshouse. In 2002 English Heritage opened the present garden, commissioned from the designer Neil Swanson. It includes one work of topiary for each of the 'Richmond Sixteen' (see page 30).

TOUR OF RICHMOND: WEST CURTAIN WALL

8 Chapel, Chapel Chamber and Great Chamber

The building of this range in about 1300 may have been prompted by a fire (see page 7), but such an expansion of the domestic apartments also reflects wider changes to lordly living, which required more and larger withdrawing chambers. Within the new range were three ground-floor rooms, the use of which is not known, and three first-floor rooms above them. A doorway in the chamber over the Cockpit entrance opened to the first of the rooms at first-floor level: the great chamber. A second doorway, knocked through a window at the east end of Scolland's Hall, would also have linked to the first-floor chambers via an external gallery, to which stairs from the bailey led up in line with the north wall of the chapel (remains of the stair can be seen in the ground).

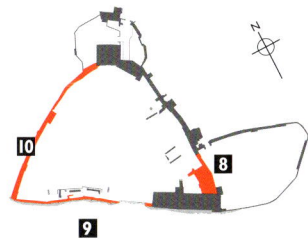

The great chamber is so identified in a survey of 1538 (see page 26). It was space for entertaining privileged guests. Beyond this was the chapel, the south wall of which preserves its piscina (a fixed basin for washing liturgical instruments) and beside it a small internal window, or squint, opening onto the great chamber. The squint enabled those in the great chamber to follow chapel services. The line of the chapel floor, and the sockets for the joists that supported it, are clearly visible in the masonry. Beyond the chapel was a third chamber of uncertain function known from the 1538 survey simply as the 'chapel chamber'. Only one wall of this last structure survives. Clearly visible in the masonry are sockets for its floor timbers.

Below: A 13th-century piscina found at Richmond. It would have been fixed into a niche in one of the castle chapels, possibly the greater chapel in the south-west corner

Bottom: The south wall of the chapel adjoining the great chamber. A piscina survives in the niche, and to its right are the remains of a squint, which allowed Mass to be observed from the great chamber next door

9 SOUTH CURTAIN WALL

On the south side of the bailey, along the edge of the cliff, are the foundations of several medieval buildings. No more specific date is known for these buildings, nor anything of their function, with one exception: somewhere in this area, probably towards the turret at the south-west corner, was the chapel known as the greater chapel and alongside it the living quarters for its community of six chaplains, supplied by Egglestone Abbey about 10 miles (16km) away. This foundation is first recorded in a grant dated 1278. The chapel and its adjoining buildings were recorded as being in decay in the 1538 survey, the roofs, walls and doors all needing repair.

10 WEST CURTAIN WALL

The south-west corner turret and the raised archway further along the west curtain wall are features visible in early drawings of the castle, but both have been heavily restored. These may originally have formed the belfry and the west window of the greater chapel.

In 1855 a barrack block was built along the full length of the west curtain wall for the then tenants of the castle, the North York Militia (see page 28). It was demolished in 1931 but its foundations in the lawn are visible in dry weather.

13

TOUR OF RICHMOND: KEEP, OR GREAT TOWER

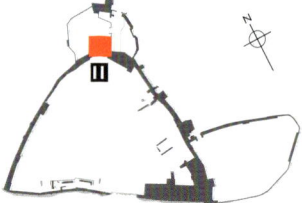

KEEP, OR GREAT TOWER

From the Norman Conquest onwards the greatest castles in England were dignified by huge stone towers, characteristically rectangular in plan and with massively thick walls. These were buildings far beyond the means of all but the greatest magnates and were intended as much as expressions of power and wealth as to serve any practical function. They were known in the 12th century simply as 'great towers'. The example at Richmond was probably built in the 1160s by Alan Rufus's great-nephew, Conan, Duke of Brittany (see page 19), and can be compared in points of design to other royal towers in the north of England at Bamburgh and Carlisle.

To contemporaries the scale of this building, which rises just over 100ft (30m) – the benchmark height of a medieval skyscraper – and has four storeys, would have been astonishing. The whole structure gives an impression of solidity and strength. Its walls rise from a sloping plinth and are articulated with thin vertical strips of stone. Small windows pierce the walls and at each corner of the battlemented parapet is a turret. The interior seems to have been designed for the formal reception of visitors rather than as a residence, as there are no kitchen services. In the late 13th century some alterations were made to the tower internally (see page 15), and the present floors were added when the building was most recently restored, in 1854–5.

Early Gateway and Ground Floor

At ground-floor level the keep contains a stretch of the original 11th-century curtain wall and principal entrance to the castle. The entrance archway is ornamented on both sides by shafts,

Below: Richmond Castle from the south. Along the cliff edge are the remains of the south curtain wall. On the other side of the bailey is the keep, dominating the skyline

TOUR OF RICHMOND: KEEP, OR GREAT TOWER

Above: The vaulting of the ground floor of the keep was added in the 13th century, probably by Edward I; the massive central pillar was designed to accommodate the well
Left: The ground floor of the keep in about 1828, before the collapsing vaults were repaired (an engraving by William Cooke of a drawing by Nathaniel Whittock)
Below: The main entrance to the keep. Its Romanesque 'cushion' capitals originally surmounted columns to either side. Throughout the keep semicircular panels over doorways denote thoroughfares

an unusual enrichment, with capitals at the head of each shaft carved to evoke Roman forms. This treatment is paralleled in the entrance to Scolland's Hall, built at the same time, and in other 11th-century work at York Minster and Durham Cathedral. There may also have been a carved panel, or tympanum, filling the semicircular section of the gateway.

In the late 13th century the ground floor was vaulted, the central column housing the well beneath it. At the same time the small spiral stair was added, giving access to the upper floors of the tower. Early 19th-century views of this interior show that the vault had by then partially collapsed; its present condition reflects considerable 19th-century reconstruction.

Entrance and First Floor

The main entrance to the keep remains today, as originally, through a doorway framed beneath a semicircular arch at wall-walk level. It opens onto a small lobby containing two further doorways. The doorway to the left leads onto a straight staircase rising to the next floor, and that on the right

TOUR OF RICHMOND: KEEP, OR GREAT TOWER

Above: The well-lit first floor of the keep, with its massive supporting column set above the ground-floor vaulting. The window sills originally reached nearly to the floor

Below: The keep from the north, the three windows of its first floor overlooking the town and market place spreading out from its base

to a large chamber that fills the volume of the tower. The central column, part of the late 13th-century alterations, is set on the ground-floor vault below and supports the ceiling, which must before then have been supported on massive transverse timbers.

Lighting the north side of the room are three windows; the sills originally dropped almost to the floor, but they were built up in the 1850s. Externally these windows are ornamented with columns, capitals and arches, that at the centre distinguished from those flanking it by a tympanum in the overarch. These windows may have served the same purpose as the balconies of other 12th-century keeps (such as at Dover and Newcastle), which allowed the lord of the castle to appear before his people assembled in the market place below. The cut stone blocks that originally covered the internal walls of this space have in places been stripped away and were replaced in the 1850s with coarse rubble masonry. To either end of this large interior are smaller vaulted rooms within the depth of the walls. Their function is unclear.

Lobby and Second Floor

The stairs from the entrance lobby are set within the depth of the keep wall. At their head is a second lobby, also within the depth of the wall. It had a large window (now partly blocked), its decorative arch a distinct feature on the exterior wall of the keep. Beneath it are the remains of a stone bench, suggesting that this space served as a waiting room for visitors to the main chamber beyond it. This main chamber is a magnificent hall rising to an open timber roof (a modern reconstruction).

TOUR OF RICHMOND: CELLS

At each end of the hall are high windows with sills stepped to allow more light to fall into the space below. This splendid interior was presumably a space for formal gatherings and audiences. Its walls of cut stone give an impression of the overall quality of the keep when it was first built.

There are four doorways on this floor. Two are topped by arches, two are not. The two that are not lead to small mural chambers that may have served as withdrawing spaces for privileged visitors. A notable feature of the keep is how architectural details signal use: semicircular overarches occur only above doors that form part of the principal internal thoroughfare of the building. Originally all such doors in the keep had these overarches. Doors to dead-ends – for example to latrines and mural chambers – have simple square heads.

The second overarched door leads to the stairs to the roof. From outside, the progress of the stairways can be tracked in the regular distribution of narrow windows following the angle of the stairs.

Roof

From the roof parapets there are splendid views over the town and surrounding country. From here it is also possible to get a clear impression of the original arrangement of the roof. The timbers of the present structure (built in the 1850s and re-leaded in 1958) are inserted into the sockets of the original roof. They form a truncated gable. The original roof, by contrast, rose to a ridge beam, supported by a projecting block of stone at each end; these stones can be seen a little below the level of the walkway.

The roof is countersunk, sitting within the top storey of the tower rather than being raised on the heads of the walls, a nearly universal form of roof among keeps in England. Above the roofline in the east wall is a narrow window, its purpose a mystery. Diagonally opposite it is a blocked doorway, reached from the stairway to the roof, which would have allowed access to service the gutters.

12 CELLS

Over the castle entrance and against the inside face of the wall beside the keep is a range of purpose-built cells constructed by 1878 for the North York Militia, then occupants of the castle. At this time there were also detention cells and a guardroom on the ground-floor of the keep. The cell block was used in 1916, during the First World War, to hold conscientious objectors (see page 30). The cell walls are covered in graffiti, much of it made by the conscientious objectors, and some made later by others who made use of these rooms or who were detained here, such as soldiers undergoing punishment during the Second World War. Due to the delicate state of these drawings there is at present no public access to the cells.

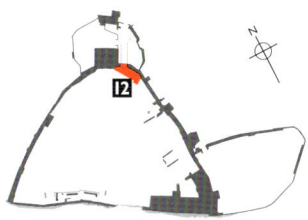

Below: The second floor of the keep formed a hall, probably used for formal gatherings and entertainments. The plain doorway on the left opens onto a mural chamber; that on the right, marked by an overarch, leads up to the roof

Bottom: The second-floor doorway to the stairway to the first floor. Through it can be seen a stone bench below the window, which provided a small waiting area for visitors

17

History of Richmond

HISTORY OF RICHMOND: BUILDING OF THE KEEP: c.1160

THE FIRST CASTLE: c.1071–1093

The exact circumstances of the foundation of Richmond remain obscure. One 12th-century poem credits William the Conqueror (r.1066–87) with building the castle in 1068–9, but there is no evidence for this. Much more probable is the late medieval tradition that it was founded by Alan Rufus, one of William's right-hand men (see page 10). Alan was granted the estates of Earl Edwin of Mercia in what is now Yorkshire after 1071 and reputedly built the castle to protect his lands from the dispossessed Anglo-Saxon nobility of the region.

Certainly by the time of the survey in 1086 known as Domesday Book, Alan had built a castle somewhere on his lands, which are described as forming a 'castelry', or an estate organized to sustain a castle. The survey also names Richmond (then called Hindrelag) as Alan's possession, and as Richmond came to form the centre of his estates it was doubtless Richmond Castle that he had built.

As far as we know the castle was built on a virgin site and, like most Norman castles, was laid out together with a new settlement. All the 11th-century fabric appears to be of one build. Four charters allow us to date this period of building more accurately: their combined evidence indicates that the castle chapel – probably that dedicated to St Nicholas in Robin Hood Tower – was given to St Mary's Abbey, York, by Alan Rufus in 1088 or 1089. The chapel, and therefore the rest of the 11th-century castle, must have existed before 1089, which implies that Richmond and its settlement were designed much as they appear today, as a walled enclosure.

Above: This crudely carved head would have adorned one of the first castle buildings at Richmond

Below: Seal impression of Conan IV, Duke of Brittany and Earl of Richmond. By his late teens he had succeeded in claiming and uniting both his vast inheritances

Facing page: William the Conqueror granting Alan Rufus the Honour of Richmond. William hands the kneeling Alan a charter with a green seal; from the Register of the Honour of Richmond, c.1400

BUILDING OF THE KEEP: c.1160

After the death of Alan Rufus in 1093, Richmond descended in turn to two of his younger brothers – Alan Niger, 'the Black' (d.1098), and Stephen. At Stephen's death in 1136 it passed to his younger son, another Alan (c.1100–1146), who was the first to style himself Earl of Richmond. Alan married Bertha, the heiress of Conan III, Duke of Brittany (d.1148). Their son Conan IV (c.1135–1171) was a minor when his father died in 1146, but during the 1150s he succeeded in claiming and uniting his two vast inheritances of Richmond and Brittany.

Conan began to assert control over his English lands from 1154. He spent considerable time at Richmond over the next decade, overseeing its administration and resolving disputes between his officials, tenants and vassals, such as that between the then constable, Roald, and one Richard de Rollos over the

HISTORY OF RICHMOND: CONSTANCE AND THE CROWN

Above: Reconstruction of Richmond Castle in about 1400, with Conan's keep in the foreground. A deer park may have occupied the bowl of the valley beyond

constableship of Richmond. Conan was a generous patron of the abbeys and priories associated with the Honour, including Easby. It was almost certainly during this period that he built the keep of Richmond, a statement of his exceptional power and wealth. He may well have begun work on it in 1160, the year of his marriage to Margaret, sister of Malcolm IV, King of Scotland.

Shortly before this prestigious match Conan also secured the Duchy of Brittany. For Conan and his successors into the 14th century the combination of the English earldom and the French duchy was difficult to manage, demanding a division of time on both sides of the Channel and, quite as important, allegiance to both kings. When these monarchs were at war it proved impossible.

CONSTANCE AND THE CROWN

Conan's only child and heir was Constance (c.1161–1201), whom he betrothed to Henry II's fourth son, Geoffrey, when she was five, ceding Brittany to the king as part of the deal. Constance was only nine when her father died and Henry II took control of Richmond. Royal accounts record substantial

HISTORY OF RICHMOND: ARTHUR AND KING JOHN

building works to the 'king's house' and 'the houses of Richmond' (presumably Scolland's Hall and other buildings in the castle enclosure) during the 1170s and 1180s.

Arthur (1187–1203), only son of Constance and Geoffrey, was born after Geoffrey's death in 1186. Constance assumed control of her estates, but under the eye of the king, who dictated her next marriage. She acted as advisor to her son in his efforts to take control of his inheritance from the English and French kings; but at her death Arthur was still a minor and Richmond passed to her third husband, Guy of Thouars.

ARTHUR AND KING JOHN

Guy of Thouars's control of Richmond was limited. When Arthur's uncle King John (r.1199–1216) seized the throne it was to John, not Guy, that the Constable of Richmond, Alan, paid 300 marks and three palfreys (riding horses) to assure himself and his successors the office and lands of constable. Meanwhile Arthur, as the son of King John's older brother, posed a threat as a potential claimant to the throne. Arthur was captured, along with his older sister, Eleanor, by the king, who had him murdered at Rouen in 1203 and kept Eleanor prisoner. The following year John took Richmond from Guy of Thouars, who had forfeited it when he invaded John's lands of Normandy. Eleanor remained in captivity until her death in 1241.

King John allowed Richmond to continue under the management of its constable, then Roald, son of Alan. But in 1207 the king fell out with Roald when he refused to pay his tax; Roald was stripped of his office until he paid a fine of 200 marks and four palfreys. Again, in 1215, Roald resisted the king, but this time more seriously: the north of England revolted against John and, although there is no record of a siege at Richmond, Roald must have stood against the king, for he was ousted from office and his garrison imprisoned in the castle until January 1216.

Above: *Arthur (right), the son and heir of Constance, paying homage to the King of France. Guided by his mother, Arthur spent his short life trying to gain control of his estates from the French and English kings. He was murdered by his uncle King John (detail of French manuscript, 1332–50)*

Below left: *Detail of an English manuscript of 1300–40, recording the genealogy of the kings of England. Here Henry II is shown, with his eight legitimate children. His grandchildren Arthur and Eleanor, children of his fourth son, Geoffrey, and Constance, were considered a threat by their uncle King John (far right)*

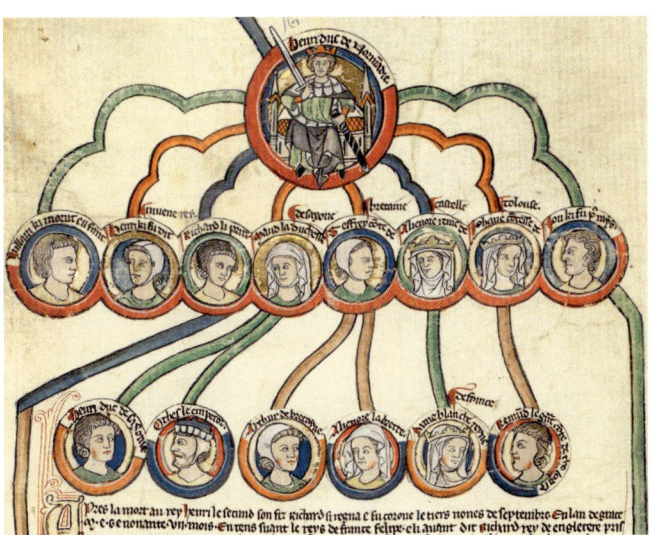

21

HISTORY OF RICHMOND: HONOUR OF RICHMOND

Honour of Richmond

Alan's vassal knights, and their successors, were bound to provide military service and castle garrison duty.

The lands granted by William the Conqueror to Alan Rufus after 1071 came to form an 'honour', a group of properties forming a single estate. Alan's honour was centred on Richmond Castle, but the title Honour of Richmond is first recorded only in 1203.

The Honour was vast: in 1086 Alan held 199 manors in Yorkshire alone, less than half the total of his landholdings. It provided the resources for building the castle and for its management and defence; subsidiary estates, taken from the Honour, were bestowed by Alan on his followers (vassals), for which they and their heirs were bound to provide a stipulated number of knights for military service and garrison duty at the castle. The value of the land was thus given in the number of 'knights' fees'. The exact terms of garrison duty are unclear, but records show that there was an annual rota of service. As well as military service, the vassals assumed formal roles in the life of the castle and the household of its lord, such as constable, chamberlain or steward. These offices passed by succession with the associated estate from heir to heir, creating a tightly knit group of families involved over many generations in the Honour. The vassals used their property within the Honour to establish castles and religious foundations of their own, while Richmond Castle formed the hub, spawning a group of lesser castles and religious institutions, including Easby Abbey.

Above: *Drawing of an effigy from Coverham Abbey, possibly of one of the Lords of Middleham, knights of the Honour of Richmond. In return for military service and guard and other duties at the castle, the knights held land in the Honour*
Right: *The heartlands of the Honour of Richmond, showing some of the principal seats of Alan's knights (see facing page)*

Facing page, bottom: *Architectural fragment from Richmond depicting a shield and cross. It may represent the arms of the chamberlain and have been placed at the east end of Scolland's Hall, the area of the castle for which he was responsible*

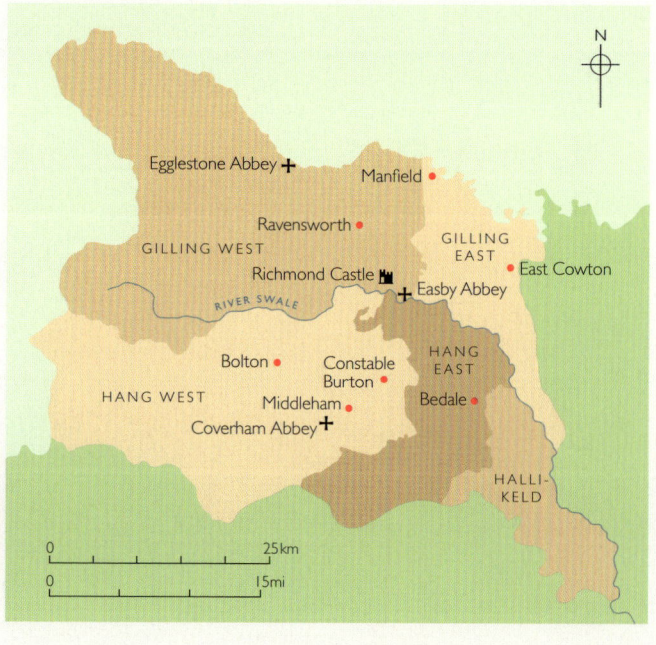

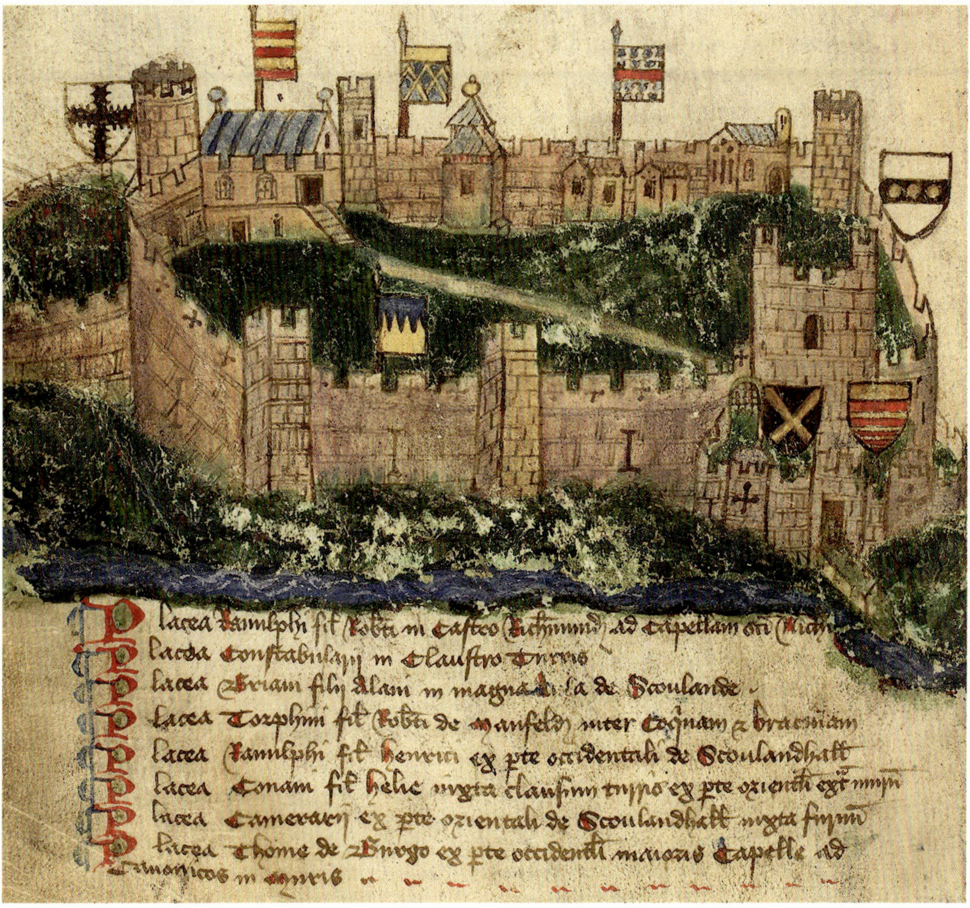

HISTORY OF RICHMOND: HONOUR OF RICHMOND

- Place of Ranulph son of Robert, in the castle of Richmond by the Chapel of St Nicholas [Ranulph FitzRobert, c.1185–1252, Lord of Middleham] 
- Place of the Constable in the enclosure of the tower [Alan, c.1140–1201, son of Roald L'Envaise the Constable, Lord of Constable Burton]
- Place of Brian son of Alan, in the great hall of Scolland [Brian FitzAlan, c.1180–1243, Lord of Bedale]  
- Place of Torphin son of Robert of Manfield, between the kitchen and brewhouse [Torphin FitzRobert, d. before 1194, Lord of Manfield]
- Place of Ranulph son of Henry, to the west of Scolland's Hall [Ranulph FitzHenry, d. before 1238, Lord of Ravensworth]  
- Place of Conan son of Ellis, beside the tower enclosure to the eastern part outside the walls [Conan FitzEllis of Cowton, c.1160–1218]
- Place of the Chamberlain to the east of Scolland's Hall beside the oven [Henry FitzConan, Lord of Kelfield] 
- Place of Thomas de Burgh, to the west of the greater chapel of the canons within the walls [Thomas de Burgh, d.c.1199, steward of Duchess Constance]

Above: Richmond Castle, from the Register of the Honour of Richmond, c.1400 (one of the earliest topographically accurate depictions of an English castle). It shows Richmond in about 1190, with the banners of the vassal knights planted above the sections of the castle defences for which each was responsible. A translation [with notes] of the caption to the drawing is given on the left

HISTORY OF RICHMOND: SHIFTING OWNERSHIP

Above: An iron sword pommel, depicting in gold, copper and enamel the arms of Peter I, Duke of Brittany and Earl of Richmond, c.1240. His arms of blue and gold check (with the ermine of Brittany in the top quarter) were retrospectively assigned to his predecessors, including Alan Rufus

Below: During the civil wars of the 1260s Richmond Castle was seized by Simon de Montfort's supporters. Whether the castle steward in charge put up a fight of the sort depicted below, or surrendered at once, is not known (detail of a French manuscript of the 1290s)

SHIFTING OWNERSHIP

Throughout the 13th and 14th centuries Richmond was generally acknowledged to be the possession of the Dukes of Brittany, but their role in international politics led to the frequent seizure of Richmond by the king. Constance's daughter by Guy de Thouars inherited after Arthur's murder. Her husband, Peter I, Duke of Brittany, ruled on in her name after her death, but his control of the Honour of Richmond was in constant dispute. By the middle decades of the 13th century Richmond was granted to a series of royal favourites. One of these, Peter of Savoy, received a royal grant of 50 oak trees towards works in the castle in 1250.

During the captivity of Henry III (r.1216–72) for a few months during the civil wars of the 1260s, Simon de Montfort effectively governed the kingdom, issuing writs in the king's name. In March and April 1265 he ordered his supporter Sir John de Deyville, Sheriff of York, to seize Richmond Castle, then the possession of the deeply royalist Peter of Savoy under his steward, Guiscard de Charrun.

Deyville was instructed 'to assume all the effective force of the aforesaid country to yourselves, to capture the aforesaid castle as seems best ... and to lay siege both strongly and firmly, so that the rebels in the aforesaid castle fortifications are unable to leave in order to inflict any damage on our faithful people'. Frustratingly, no details of the siege, if indeed there was one, are recorded. De Montfort was killed in August 1265 and the king briefly restored Richmond to Peter of Savoy.

In May 1266 Henry III returned Richmond to the Dukes of Brittany, granting it to Peter I's son John I (c.1217–1286), who had long petitioned for its return. John I immediately resigned it to his son John II (1239–1305), who went on to fight in the Crusades. In 1278, having returned to Europe, John II made an agreement with Egglestone Abbey to provide a community of six chaplains for the greater chapel in the castle (see page 13).

HISTORY OF RICHMOND: REPAIRS OF EDWARD I

Above: The funeral of John III in 1341, his coffin draped in a pall of ermine, the emblem of the Dukes of Brittany (detail of a French manuscript of 1410–18)

Left: The ground floor of Richmond keep. The great vaults were probably inserted by Edward I, after he seized the castle from the Duke of Brittany upon the outbreak of war with France in 1294

Below: Humberware jugs found at the castle, dating from 1450 to 1550. These were utilitarian vessels, appropriate for serving beer

REPAIRS OF EDWARD I

When war broke out with France in 1294 and John II sided with the French king, Edward I (r.1272–1307) seized Richmond. He immediately began repairs to the castle, probably including the insertion of the ground-floor vault in the keep, the raising of the mural towers and work to the domestic range beside Scolland's Hall. Planks were also obtained to repair the drawbridge. During these works the castle was used to hold hostages of the war and also, in 1295, to accommodate the wife of Miles de Stapleton, who was travelling to Gascony on the king's business.

Edward I's investment in the castle preceded his first invasion of Scotland in 1296. John II's second son, also John (d.1334), played a prominent role in the ensuing Anglo-Scottish wars and in 1305 (after his father's death) was made Guardian of Scotland by Edward I. A year later he was restored to the Earldom and Honour of Richmond, while his elder brother held Brittany. He may have made improvements to the castle, though no record of these survives. The town walls enclosing the market place were probably built by him after Edward II granted him 'murage' – a toll on all goods brought to the town for building and repairing the town walls. His nephew, John III of Brittany (1312–41), inherited the Honour.

John III died childless in 1341. A survey was taken for the king, which records the dilapidated state of the castle and town: 'At Richmond there is a castle, whose land inside the walls is worth nothing, nor the land in the castle ditch, and

HISTORY OF RICHMOND: RICHMOND UNDER THE TUDORS

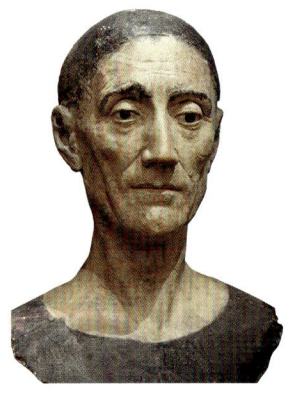

Top: Richmond Castle by Francis Place, c.1670. Along the curtain wall in line with the keep are the remains of what was probably the greater chapel
Above: The funeral effigy of Henry VII, who built Richmond Palace at Sheen, naming it after the earldom of his father, Edmund Tudor
Below: Henry Fitzroy, illegitimate son of Henry VIII, was made by his father Duke of Richmond and Somerset; portrait miniature by Lucas Horenbout

whose buildings and walls are badly in need of repair.' It was in this condition that Richmond was granted by Edward III (r.1327–77) to one of his younger sons, John of Gaunt. It passed back to the Dukes of Brittany in 1372 and in 1399 was resumed by Henry IV (r.1399–1413) as a Crown possession.

RICHMOND UNDER THE TUDORS

In 1452 the Lancastrian Henry VI (r.1422–61; 1470–71) created his half-brother Edmund Tudor Earl of Richmond. Ten years later, during the dynastic struggle for the Crown known as the Wars of the Roses, Richmond passed in sequence to the two brothers of the Yorkist Edward IV (r.1461–70; 1471–83): Richard, Duke of Gloucester (later Richard III), and George, Duke of Clarence. Whether either occupied the castle is not known. The earldom, however, was inherited by Edmund's son, Henry Tudor, who was forced into exile. In 1485 he secured the Crown at the Battle of Bosworth and became England's first Tudor monarch, Henry VII (r.1485–1509), and the Honour again became a possession of the Crown.

Some years later the name of Richmond was revived in an unexpected way. In 1497 Henry VII's principal palace at Sheen, Surrey, on the river Thames was burnt down. He had it rebuilt in 1501 and renamed Richmond after his title as earl. The prestige of the name is again apparent in the choice of the title Duke of Richmond and Somerset by Henry VIII (r.1509–47) for his illegitimate son Henry Fitzroy in 1525.

Yet despite the value placed on the name, the Yorkshire castle languished. During the invasion scare of 1538 Henry VIII had several northern castles surveyed, including Richmond. John, Lord Scrope, and Christopher, Lord Conyers, made their report for the king of the ruinous Richmond: 'masonry, timber, and iron needed for the Port Lodge, the inner gate house, the sware [square] house, the mantill wall and five turrets, the great dongion, two wells, the hall, pantry, buttery, kitchen, and

HISTORY OF RICHMOND: THE CASTLE IN RUIN

other offices, the privy chamber, a little tower for draughtes, the great chamber, and a chapel next it, the chapel in the castle garth, &c. The circuit of the mantill wall is 2,000 ft. There are no guns or artillery.'

THE CASTLE IN RUIN

The parlous state of the castle as described in 1538 was corroborated in about 1540 by the antiquarian John Leland, who described it as 'in mere ruine'. For the next 300 years the castle was left to languish. Ownership meanwhile passed in 1675 to the Dukes of Richmond, the title having been revived by Charles II (r.1660–85) for his illegitimate son Charles Lennox (1672–1723), whose heirs continue to own the castle.

Views of the castle in the 1680s show that little has changed since then, though some of its cliff-top buildings collapsed in about 1720, when 'a curious horn and a large silver spoon' were found in the rubble and sent to the Duke of Richmond. About this time antiquarian interest in the castle began to revive with the publication in 1722 of a transcript of the Register of the Honour of Richmond of about 1400. There was also some casual exploration of the ruins. In 1785 the antiquary Francis Grose noted: 'In 1732, Mr Wharton of Newcastle, agent to the late duke, causing some rubbish to be removed, discovered a drawbridge and moat, belonging to the castle, of very curious workmanship.' He produced a plan of the castle and annotated the area behind the keep as being the former site of buildings.

In 1745 the 2nd Duke of Richmond considered doing repairs, which were apparently later carried out by his son, the 3rd Duke, in 1761–5, when repairs costing £350 were made to the keep, the Cockpit garden and other dilapidated parts. Despite this work, by 1814 the castle was described in a guide to the town as 'a striking memorial of worldly instability'.

Above: The illegitimate son of Charles II, Charles Lennox, for whom the king revived the title of Duke of Richmond in 1675. His heirs continue to own the castle today

Below: Richmond Castle from the west by Paul Sandby and William Taverner in about 1750, at the time the 2nd Duke of Richmond was considering doing some repairs

27

HISTORY OF RICHMOND: VICTORIAN BARRACKS

VICTORIAN BARRACKS

The castle's period of abandonment and ruin came to an end in 1854, when the Duke of Richmond leased it to what was then the County of the North Riding. The following year it became the headquarters of the North York Militia. The keep was completely restored: the 11th-century entrance arch was unblocked (see page 4), the ground-floor vault repaired, and the present floors and roofs inserted. A castellated barrack block was built along the length of the west curtain wall and a cell block beside the castle gate (see page 17).

An 1897 Richmondshire guidebook described the results of these changes: 'The lower storey of the Castle Keep is now used as a Guard Room of the 4th Battalion Yorkshire Regiment, while the apartments above are fitted up as an armoury, where arms and accoutrements are kept for about 700 men. Some forty years ago the area within the walls was levelled for a parade ground and a number of dwellings were built in keeping with the castle, to accommodate sixteen of the staff sergeants of the Regiment. The terrace walk outside the walls was also constructed.'

Top: The barracks inside the west curtain wall in June 1931, shortly before demolition. They provided married quarters; the unmarried soldiers were billeted in the town
Above: A 19th-century military button, found at Richmond Castle
Below right: Children – possibly of soldiers stationed here – playing in the castle bailey in about the 1880s. The lines chalked in the grass would have been for military drill
Below: A pewter tankard found at the castle. Its maker's mark dates it to 1860–83, when the North York Militia was stationed here

28

HISTORY OF RICHMOND: A PRISON AND A MONUMENT

A PRISON AND A MONUMENT

The castle became the headquarters of the Northumbrian division of the Territorial Army in 1908. The Army officer and hero of the Boer War (and later founder of the Boy Scouts) Robert Baden-Powell (1857–1941) commanded the division from 1908 to 1910. When at Richmond he lived in 'the tower' – the officers' quarters at the south end of the castle barracks.

In 1910 parts of the castle came into the guardianship of the then Office of Works and a campaign began to restore the buildings. Spoil from levelling the parade ground in front of the barracks had been piled against the eastern wall, which was threatening to collapse. This was cleared and some medieval foundations were revealed in the process. Military fittings from the keep were stripped out and the walls of the buildings repaired and repointed.

The Cockpit was 'cut up into allotment gardens and the area outside the eastern wall was disfigured with pigsties, chicken runs and rubbish heaps', Sir Charles Peers recorded in the first official guidebook to the site in 1953. But eventually all this was cleared away. Throughout this work the castle remained in military occupation. Following the outbreak of the First World War it became, in May 1916, a base for the newly created Northern Non-Combatant Corps, some of whom were imprisoned in the cell block (see page 30).

The Victorian barracks was demolished in 1931 and the whole site was thereafter given into the care of the State. During the Second World War the military again took over the castle. Temporary wash-houses and latrines were built; the keep was used as an air-raid shelter and its roof as a lookout. Again the cell block was used as a prison, this time for regular soldiers undergoing punishment. The castle is now in the care of the English Heritage Trust.

Below left: The arched gateway from the Cockpit, looking out towards the eastern ditch, in 1913; it was in such a state of decay that the Office of Works took over guardianship of much of the castle in 1910

Audit Money
In 1576 Elizabeth I granted Richmond its first Royal Charter of Incorporation (power of self-government) and a portion of Crown rent was set aside for the poor. The giving out of this 'Audit Money' by the mayor has taken place ever since. In 1821 it was still paid 'about Christmas to poor tradesmen, decayed housekeepers, and other indigent persons of the town'. Today it is given to residents over the age of 60, though it is no longer legal currency or funded by the Crown. In 1986 the 'Richmond Shilling' was minted to pay it. On one face are the Richmond arms with, in Latin, 'The mother of all Richmonds. Queen Elizabeth 1576'. On the other is a view of the castle.

29

HISTORY OF RICHMOND: CELL BLOCK AND THE 'SIXTEEN'

Right: Eleven of the 'Richmond Sixteen' among the COs photographed here at Dyce Camp, near Aberdeen, in 1916, where they were sent to serve part of their sentence of hard labour for refusal to fight. Bert Brocklesby is third row from the front, far right
Below: Annie Wainwright, as drawn by her fiancé, Bert Brocklesby, on his cell wall at Richmond in 1916
Bottom: The upper corridor of the cell block today

Cell Block and the 'Richmond Sixteen'

The walls of the cell block are covered with a remarkable survival: the graffiti of men confined here over the course of the 20th century.

The graffiti include a portrait by one of the conscientious objectors (COs), also dubbed 'conchies', held here in 1916 of his fiancée, a sketch of the Luftwaffe, and the scrawl of three young men confined in 1940 as 'drunk and disorderly'.

Perhaps most poignant of the survivals are the records of the COs. Eighteen months into the First World War, in March 1916, the Government introduced conscription in response to appalling casualty rates and the decline in volunteers. Men could appeal against military service on conscientious grounds, but unless these COs received full exemption they were obliged to enter the Non-Combatant Corps (NCC): a uniformed branch of the Army subject to military discipline. In May 1916 Richmond Castle became the northern base for the corps.

Some of the COs, however, refused to be involved in any Army activity at all, including drill, wearing uniform or work related to the war effort. Bert Brocklesby, for example, was asked if he would serve in a munitions factory or sweep mines. He refused, saying 'they would not let me sweep English mines as well as German mines'. These

HISTORY OF RICHMOND: CELL BLOCK AND THE 'SIXTEEN'

COs were considered in breach of military discipline, court-martialled and punished. A small number were imprisoned at Richmond in the cell block beside the keep (see page 17), where some, including Brocklesby, left a record of their presence, and courage, on the walls in pencil.

Many were Nonconformists and their graffiti devotional; Brocklesby wrote in his cell in May 1916: 'Every cross grows light beneath the shadow Lord of Thine'. Herbert Green wrote: 'Brought into this cell after being court martialled at the Castle, Richmond. No surrender! No Conscription!'; another left a message to those who would come after him: 'All COs who enter here be of good cheer for we cannot lose in this fight for liberty, for Right ever came out on top.'

The authorities decided to make an example of 16 of the COs at Richmond by sending them to France, where the penalty for refusal to obey orders in the face of the enemy was death. The so-called Richmond Sixteen were taken from the castle on 29 May 1916 and sent to a camp near Boulogne. Desperate attempts were made by their friends in England to discover their whereabouts. A doctored field postcard sent by Brocklesby informed them and the situation immediately became an embarrassment to the Army.

In June the Sixteen were court-martialled and taken to a parade ground to hear their sentences. As one recalled, 'The army authorities then made a great show of the proceedings … The proper soldiers were all lined up so many deep to make 3 sides of a large square. At the 4th side of the square was erected a large raised platform. We were led up on to this platform and a high ranking officer read out our crime and the punishment.' The sentence was given: 'death by shooting', then – after a pause – commuted to 10 years of hard labour. They were returned to Britain to serve their sentence, but all were released by summer 1919.

Over the next 70 years the cells at Richmond housed many others who left their marks on the walls. Among them were soldiers detained for disciplinary reasons during the Second World War, including men from the East Yorkshire Regiment and the Green Howards (both now part of the Yorkshire Regiment). One, Private J.A. Thomas, recorded his detention on 11 November 1939 'for not swinging his arms' – presumably during drill.

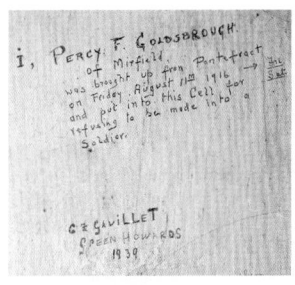

Top: A caricature of Hitler on one of the cell walls, presumably by a soldier of the Second World War undergoing disciplinary confinement
Above: 'I, Percy F. Goldsbrough of Mirfield, was brought up from Pontefract on Friday August 11th and put into this cell for refusing to be made into a soldier'
Below: Devotional sketch and words by John Hubert ('Bert') Brocklesby, 22 May 1916

31

TOUR OF EASBY: INTRODUCTION

Tour of Easby

The Premonstratensian abbey of St Agatha stands on the banks of the river Swale about a mile downstream from Richmond Castle. It was founded by Roald L'Envaise (d. before 1159), Constable of Richmond Castle, in 1151, some 70 years after the castle was built. The abbey supplanted an existing Anglo-Saxon church served by a community of priests, termed a minster. Anglo-Saxon sculpture from the minster can still be seen in the parish church beside the ruins. The new abbey that took shape over the next 150 years was laid out in a conventional medieval manner, with the monastic church and communal domestic buildings around a cloister. There survive from the 13th century a particularly fine gatehouse and monastic dining hall, or refectory. In 1319–20 the abbey passed into the patronage of the Scropes, Lords of Bolton. Several members of the family made generous bequests to the monastery and chose to be buried there.

Easby was suppressed by Henry VIII in 1536–7 and its history thereafter is poorly documented. Some of its buildings, notably the gatehouse and mill, remained in use. Others appear to have been stripped and fell into ruin. In the early 18th century a fine house was built overlooking the abbey and in about 1820 its owner began to clear the ruins for picturesque effect. Thereafter Easby began to attract antiquarians and tourists.

Limited repairs were made to the ruins in the 1850s, but it was not until 1886 that the site was excavated. The ruins passed into State guardianship in the 1930s and are now in the care of the English Heritage Trust.

Above: *View of Easby Abbey from the east, looking towards the great refectory window on the left and the church remains at centre right*
Below: *The 12th-century font in the parish church of Easby*

Facing page: *The magnificent south front of the guest hall in the west range would have overlooked the entrance forecourt of the abbey*

33

TOUR OF EASBY: OVERVIEW AND SETTING

EASBY ABBEY

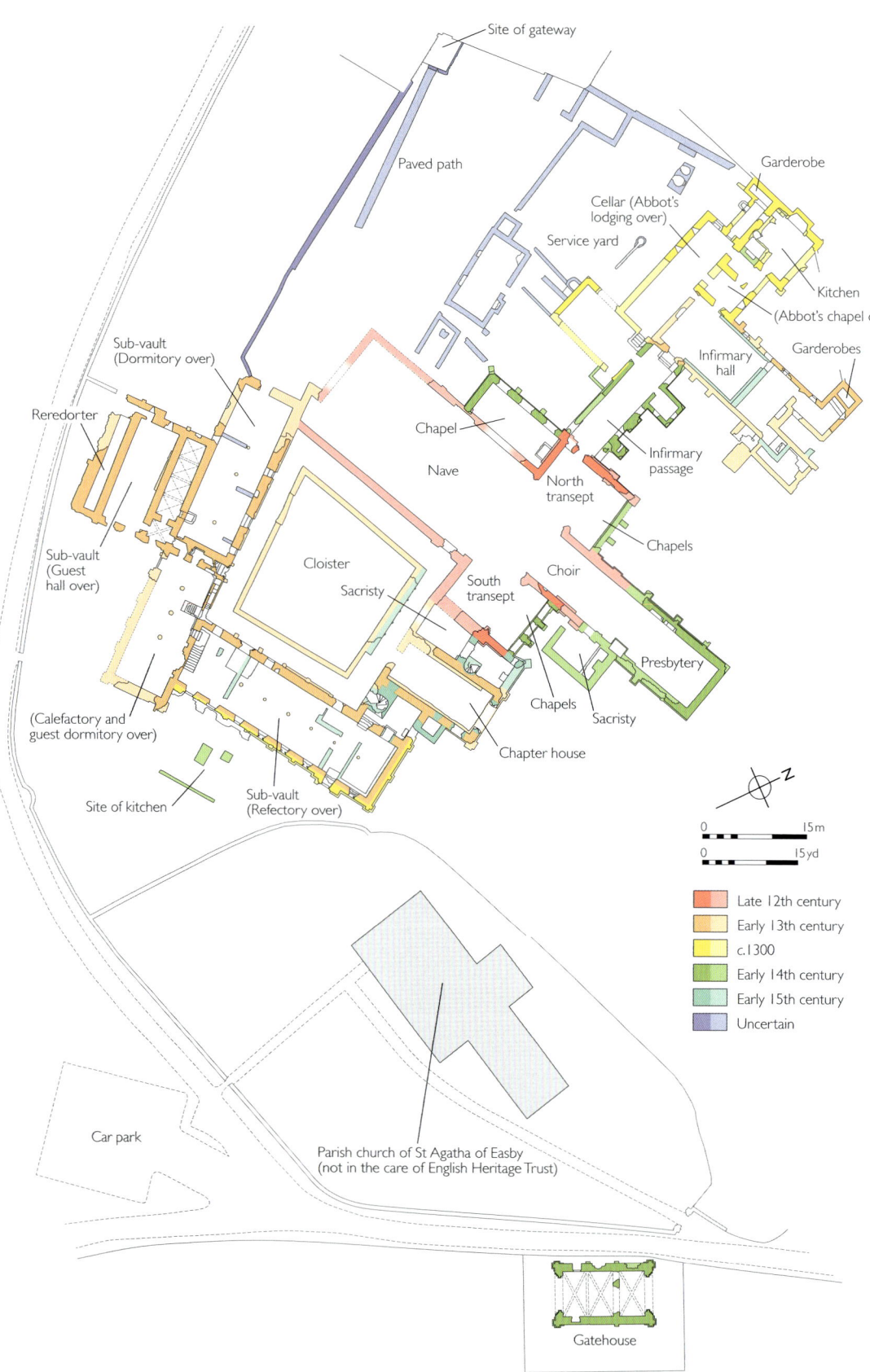

TOUR OF EASBY: OVERVIEW AND SETTING

OVERVIEW AND SETTING

Easby was the third Premonstratensian abbey established in England and the first of three in the Honour of Richmond. It was followed by Coverham (founded at Swainby by 1187 and transferred in 1212 to the banks of the Cover, near Middleham Castle) and Egglestone (founded between 1195 and 1198). Easby subsumed a minster, or community of priests, that had probably been there since the 8th century. The rebuilt parish church of St Agatha may stand on the site of the minster.

Roald's initial endowment was probably enough only to begin the abbey church, with temporary domestic buildings to support the community. Further bequests in the late 12th century enabled building to continue. Most of the ruins seen today are of buildings created during the 13th century.

The abbey stands on the north side of a shallow valley that drops to the river Swale. Originally a high wall encircled the abbey grounds, or precinct, which was much larger than the present site and included to the south, beyond the church car park, a barn or granary (the remains are not currently accessible) and to the north on the river a mill (now in private ownership). To the east is the gatehouse, the principal entrance to the precinct. The abbey ruins constitute three main areas: the community's living quarters (conventual buildings), which enclose three sides of the cloister; the abbey church, enclosing the remaining (north) side of the cloister; and beyond that various ancillary buildings, including what were probably the abbot's house and an infirmary.

Above: A reconstruction drawing of Easby Abbey from the south-west, as it may have looked in about 1500. The southern half of the west range – seen here to the lower left – today remains only as footings in the grass

Below: Photograph of the abbey barn or granary in 1938. Originally the abbey precinct incorporated the barn to the south and the abbey mill, which lies up river to the north

35

TOUR OF EASBY: GATEHOUSE

Right: The abbey gatehouse from the south, from what would have been the inner side of the abbey precinct
Below: The vaulted passageway through the gatehouse from the north, with its large archway for wagons, and its small archway for those on foot. On this, outer, side the canons would have distributed alms to the poor
Below right: The abbey in the late 18th century by Samuel Hieronymus Grimm. The wall in the foreground probably formed one of several subdivisions within the monastic precinct; it is now gone, as is the gatehouse roof
Bottom: Architectural detail on the outer archway of the gatehouse. Faint traces of the red and white paint that originally decorated the interior can still be seen

◧ GATEHOUSE

Today the site is accessed through a gate off the path to the west, above the river, but originally the main entrance was via the two-storey gatehouse to the east. The gatehouse survived in use after the Reformation as a granary and was stripped of its post-medieval accretions, including a roof, by the Office of Works in the 1930s. The scale and ornament of this building, with its tall, richly carved windows, declared to the outside world the status of its own chambers and the dignity of the abbey in general.

The gatehouse served two functions. The ground floor forms a passageway, vaulted, and divided by a cross-wall containing two archways: a large one for vehicles and a small one for those on foot. The archways carried gates (the holes for the fittings are visible). The area on the outer side of the gates functioned as a covered porch, where alms would have been distributed to the poor.

TOUR OF EASBY: WEST RANGE

The first-floor chamber was reached by an outer stairway, leading from within the precinct. It may have served as a court room or counting house, administrative interiors often found in gatehouses. On either side of the gatehouse were originally lean-to buildings, including a porter's lodge; the doors and rooflines of these buildings remain in the sides of the gatehouse.

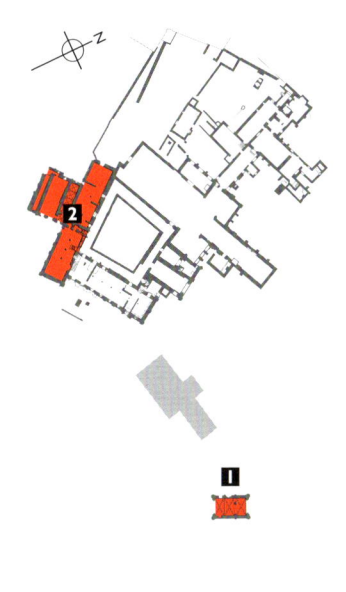

2 WEST RANGE

The west range overlooked what was the outer court of the abbey, a yard for the monastery's service buildings. The two lower storeys of the range were vaulted throughout, supporting the floor of the chambers above. The main section of the range consisted of a long, three-storey building, its north half enclosing the cloister and its south half the west end of the refectory. The southern half has collapsed, leaving only foundations visible in the grass. This main range was built against the rising hill of the river valley, so that its first floor led out at ground-floor level onto the cloister. Within the second floor – now largely lost – was the monastic dormitory. Here the canons' beds were arranged along the sides of the interior. By the time of the Dissolution it is likely that each would have been enclosed by timber screens or fabric tents for privacy.

Projecting behind the main range towards the river was another three-storey building, most of which survives. Nearest the river is the reredorter, or main latrines, with doors at all three levels. Latrines were probably ranged along the length of the upper two floors, the wider first floor accommodating the drains from the latrines above. A single latrine may have existed

Below: The north section of the west range, nearest the river. At the far left are the abbey latrines (the reredorter) and at the centre, at first-floor level, is the guest hall

TOUR OF EASBY: REFECTORY

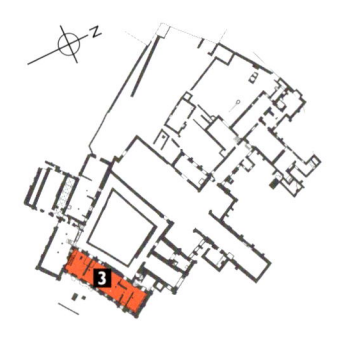

Below: The hatch (centre) in the south wall of the refectory. Servants passed food through the hatch from the kitchen outside to others waiting to serve the canons at their tables
Bottom: The grand two-storey refectory from the south

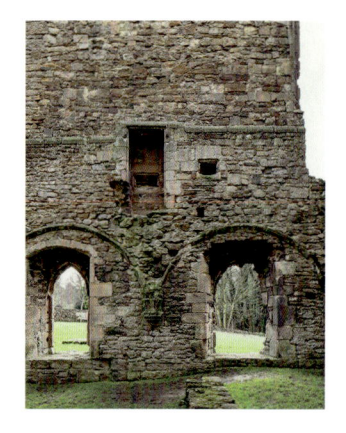

at ground-floor level. They drained into a channel flushed by water fed from the river. Beside the reredorter, at first-floor level, was the guest hall, where visitors to the abbey were entertained. The striking intersecting arches of its south windows survive, as do a fine window and seat in its north wall. The use of the other rooms of the west range is not known, though those on the ground floor probably served in part for storage, and its upper floors probably contained a heated common room (calefactory) for the canons, and a guest dormitory.

3 REFECTORY

The impressive shell of the two-storey dining hall, or refectory, encloses the south side of the cloister. Its first floor formed the dining hall, where the ritualized meals of the canons were eaten in silence to the accompaniment of reading. The ground floor was probably used for storage. The building comprises the remains of an early 13th-century structure remodelled in about 1300; the two phases of construction are apparent in the contrasting style of window tracery and in the change of level of the vault. The arches for the vault can be seen along the lower walls, with the stumps of the pillars that supported it running down the centre of the building. The vault was slightly raised in places during the works of about 1300.

The entrance to the refectory was up a staircase from the surviving door in the cloister. Dominating the hall is the huge east window (rebuilt by Sir George Gilbert Scott in 1869), which would have lit the abbot's table immediately beneath. To the right was an elevated pulpit from which a canon would

TOUR OF EASBY: THE PREMONSTRATENSIANS

The Premonstratensians

The Premonstratensians became known as the White Canons, after the colour of their habits.

The Premonstratensians take their name from their mother house in Premontré, Picardy, France, founded in about 1120 by St Norbert of Xanten (d.1134). Their community was made up of canons regular, priests living together under the religious rule of life of St Augustine, holding their property in common and with duties similar to those of monks. Unlike monks their purpose was to engage in ministry to the outside world. At the time of the order's inception they were deeply influenced by the spirituality and governance of the Cistercians, whose strict religious observance and centralized organization they combined with their service to the laity of preaching and the management of parishes.

About 30 Premonstratensian houses had been founded in England by 1267. Here the community became known as the White Canons after the colour of their habits. Curiously, in 1400 and again in 1419 the canons of Easby, who had stopped wearing the traditional tunic (rochet) under their cloaks, were licensed by Pope Boniface IX 'to wear in future within and without the cloister of their monastery linen rochets beneath their cloaks, and black hoods and caps (birettas)'.

None of the Premonstratensian houses was rich by the standards of great English monasteries. Uniquely – aside from the Carthusians – they never established themselves in the universities of Oxford or Cambridge. Perhaps as a result the order produced only one English medieval bishop. This was Richard Redman (d.1505), Abbot of Shap in Westmorland, who became in sequence Bishop of St Asaph, Exeter and finally Ely. His conscientious visitations (inspections of the Premonstratensian houses across the country) give a picture of the order over a period of 46 years during the run-up to the Reformation. In that time ten houses were regularly praised for their observance; seven, including Easby, passed through difficulties; and the remainder suffered regular breaches of monastic discipline.

Above: St Norbert (right), founder of the Premonstratensian Order, receiving the religious rules of life from St Augustine (detail of a manuscript illustration, c.1200)

Below: Reconstruction drawing of the Premonstratensian church of Shap Abbey, as it may have looked when Richard Redman (d.1505) was its abbot. The abbey church of Easby would have appeared very similar

TOUR OF EASBY: PARISH CHURCH OF ST AGATHA

Right: A section of the restored 13th-century wall paintings in the church, depicting scenes from the life of Christ

Below: The Easby Cross, depicting Christ enthroned above the figures of his apostles, now in the Victoria and Albert Museum, London. It dates from 800 to 820, and is presumably associated with the original minster, which Easby Abbey and the parish church replaced

Parish Church of St Agatha of Easby

The parish church may have been built on the site of the Anglo-Saxon minster, which the abbey supplanted.

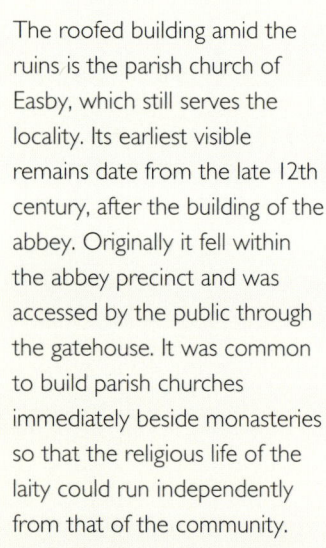

The roofed building amid the ruins is the parish church of Easby, which still serves the locality. Its earliest visible remains date from the late 12th century, after the building of the abbey. Originally it fell within the abbey precinct and was accessed by the public through the gatehouse. It was common to build parish churches immediately beside monasteries so that the religious life of the laity could run independently from that of the community.

In the chancel is a plaster copy of an 8th-century cross, part of which was reputedly discovered in a wall before 1869 and the remainder removed from the fabric of the church in 1930. It is evidence of the early importance of Easby as an ecclesiastical centre. Near the high altar are the heavily restored and fragmentary remains of a 13th-century cycle of wall paintings: those on the north wall include scenes from the Fall of Adam and Eve and those on the south scenes from the life and Passion of Christ.

On the south wall beside the high altar is a triple seat for use by the clergy, each seat painted with the figure of a bishop. Beside these is a piscina (a fixed basin for washing liturgical instruments). In the window above the high altar are fragments of medieval glass. That on the right is a figure of St John, taken from a Crucifixion scene. It can be dated by comparison with glass at York Minster to the 1180s and was almost certainly originally part of a greater window in the abbey.

The nave arcades also preserve extensive traces of medieval painted decoration, including bold chevron patterns and delicate fronds of foliage.

TOUR OF EASBY: CLOISTER AND CHAPTER HOUSE

read during meals. A stair in the depth of the wall gave access to the pulpit. Down each side of the hall were high windows decorated with stone tracery. A 14th-century law case records that these windows were glazed and decorated with coats-of-arms. The canons sat with their backs to the walls at tables ranged along the sides of the room, allowing the servants to move freely in the centre.

Food was served through a hatch in the wall immediately opposite the entrance door. In the lawn outside are the remains of the kitchen, including its central hearth. The west end of the refectory – beyond the door and service hatch – was walled off and heated with its own fire. It probably formed a subsidiary dining chamber used by the senior canons on ordinary days. Only on feast days would the whole community have eaten together.

4 CLOISTER AND 5 CHAPTER HOUSE

The cloister was the hub of the abbey. It comprised a garden enclosed on four sides by arcaded walks. Only the foundations of these walks now remain, but surviving fragments of masonry indicate that the 13th-century arcades consisted of slender columns supporting richly carved arches. A curiosity of the remaining foundations is an unusually large monolith incorporated (when is not known) into the west walk. Clearly visible in the standing walls of the enclosing refectory and west range is the horizontal scar of the pitched cloister roof. The fine dormitory door faces onto the west clositer walk and beside it is a niche for a basin, or lavabo, used by the canons to wash their hands when they processed into the refectory for meals.

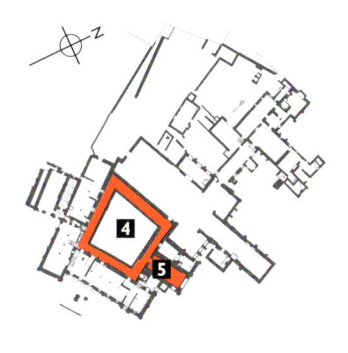

Below: The finely decorated door in the west cloister walk, which led up to the canons' dormitory on the second floor of the west range
Bottom: The chapter house, left, with its great east window. Here the canons met to hear their daily reading

TOUR OF EASBY: CHURCH

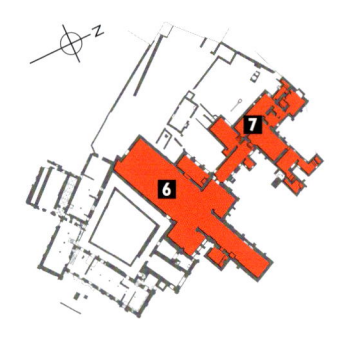

Below: Monks burying a bishop in a tomb niche (detail of an English manuscript of 1175 to 1200)

Bottom: Two tomb niches of the Scrope family in the choir, the most privileged section of the church. They preserve traces of red and white paint

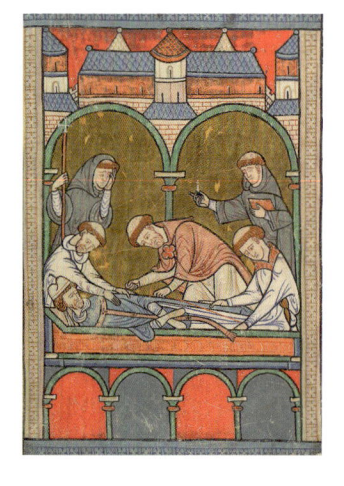

The foundations of the eastern cloister have been widened, possibly to form a bench, and ornamented with stone ribs (a detail now mostly obscured). In the centre of the east cloister range are the ruins of the chapter house, a chamber where the community met formally each day. The canons sat on stone benches around the walls. In the 15th century the chapter house and its range were refashioned and a new spiral stair inserted within it to give access to the upper floor.

The line of the east range roof is visible as a scar in the ruined refectory wall. On the outside of the range survive the remains of the late medieval whitened render finish to the buildings.

6 CHURCH

The abbey church was probably the first structure to be built after the foundation of the abbey in 1151. The church is laid out on a cross-shaped plan with a broad nave opening into a long, narrow choir. Originally the choir was shorter, but it was lengthened to the east in the early 14th century, at which time a sacristy or chapel was added to its south side. To either side of the nave are short arms, termed transepts. The transepts and the walls of a side chapel are the best-preserved elements of the building.

The choir was the site of the high altar and the area of the church reserved for the devotions of the community. Two tomb niches for patrons of the abbey survive in the north wall of this privileged space. Each canon would have sat in a seat, or stall, ranged to either side of the interior. Astonishingly, the early 16th-century stalls survive: they were almost certainly removed to the Church of St Mary in Richmond after the Dissolution, where they remain today (see pages 46–7).

TOUR OF EASBY: NORTHERN BUILDINGS

A screen surmounted with a crucifix would have divided the choir from the nave. Probably against this, as well as within the transepts and nave itself, would have stood numerous subsidiary altars. Areas of paving and several tombs survive in the nave. One block has circles faintly inscribed in the surface: each circle marks the position to be taken by a canon when the community prepared for a liturgical procession. In places the interior preserves slight traces of medieval painted decoration: red lines on a white ground.

7 NORTHERN BUILDINGS

North of the church is the infirmary hall, a space built to accommodate sick canons. This was expanded to the north and west in about 1300 to create lodgings for the abbot. In the early 14th century a two-storey corridor was built, linking this cluster of buildings to the north transept of the church. Only the footings of this corridor remain. At its north end is the door to the infirmary hall. Typically these large interior spaces formed dormitories with beds arranged along the walls. The rooms at the east end of the infirmary were perhaps created as an afterthought to offer more private accommodation.

On the north side of the hall are the remains of a chapel building. The chapel was at first-floor level, lit by a large pointed window. A piscina is visible in the wall to the right. This was presumably the abbot's chapel and opened off a lost first-floor chamber of his lodging that oversailed the corridor. Beyond the chapel are the remains of a kitchen with a large fireplace in the north wall and the bases for cooking pots in the west wall. This may have served the infirmary and the abbot's lodging. Further evidence of associated service buildings, including two stone oven bases, can be seen in the grass to the west. This service area was accessible through a small gate in the north-west corner of the precinct wall, the blocked base of which survives.

Above: The remains of the northern buildings of the abbey, seen from the north-east. The large window at the centre marks the site of the infirmary hall, where the abbey's sick canons were taken to recuperate

Below: The installation of an abbot, depicted in an English manuscript of the 1430s. At Easby the abbot's quarters were located in the northern buildings, where he had his own lodgings and a private chapel

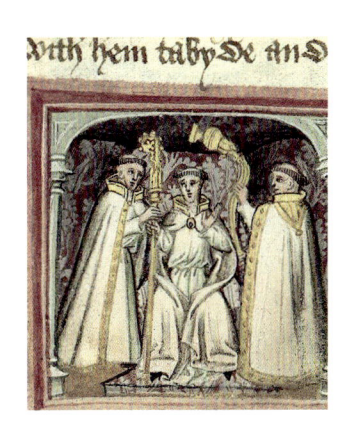

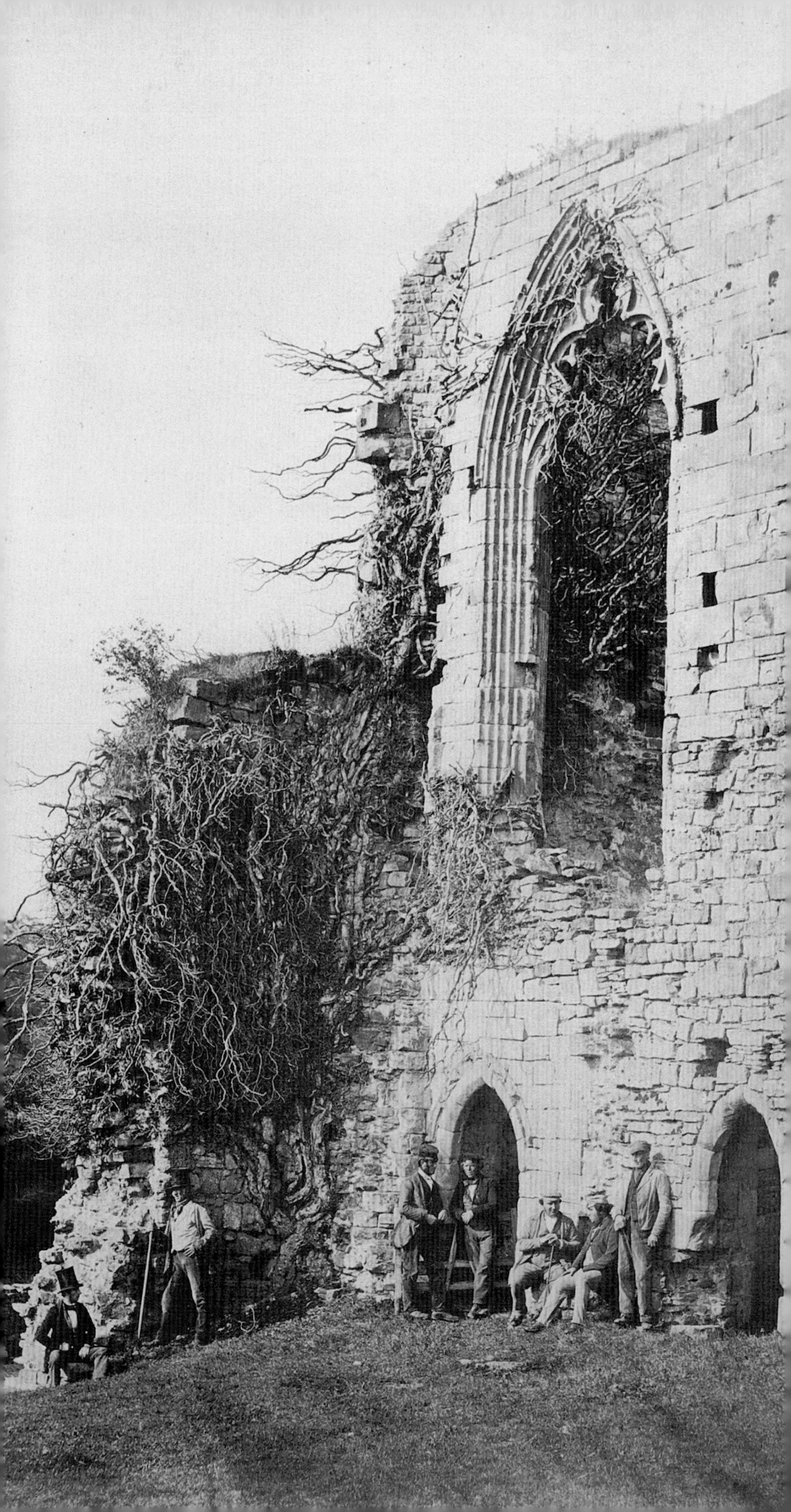

HISTORY OF EASBY: FOUNDATION OF THE ABBEY

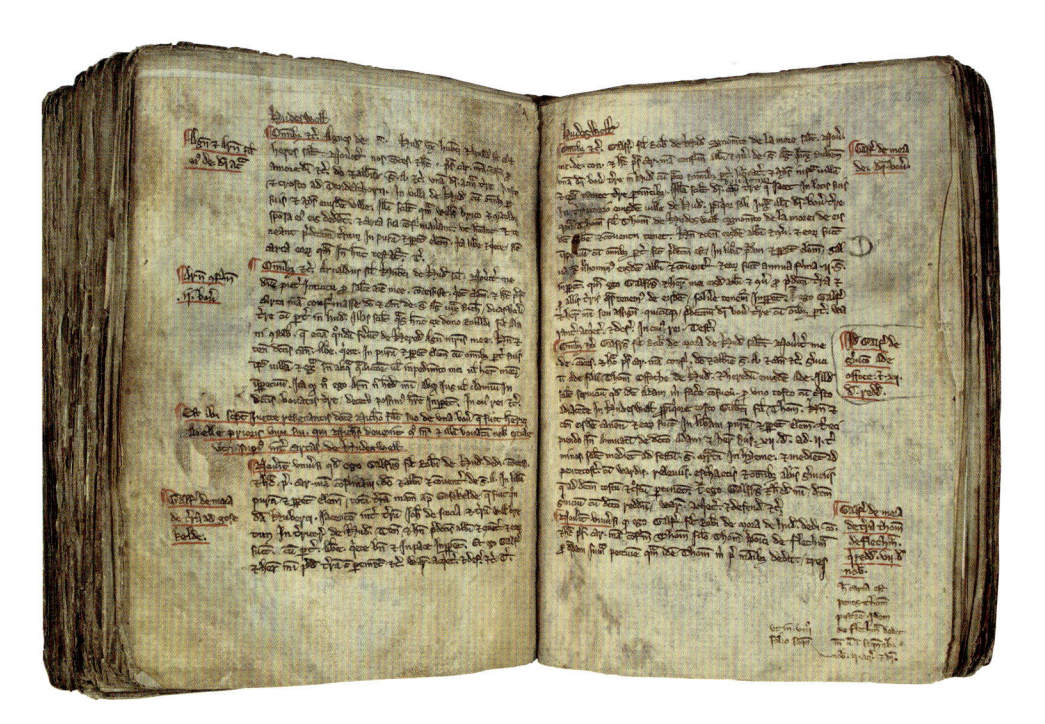

History of Easby

FOUNDATION OF THE ABBEY

In 1151 a charter issued by Roald, Constable of Richmond Castle, with the consent of his wife and son, granted the minster of Easby to God, St Mary, St Agatha and the canons of the Premonstratensian Order. He also made a small gift of land. By his office Roald was a rich and substantial landowner.

Little is certain about the minster at Easby, but it was probably a community of priests, a type of religious institution widespread in Anglo-Saxon England. During the church reforms of the 11th century such institutions were commonly recast – in effect modernized – as monastic foundations. Easby is a late example of such a transformation. The parish church may stand on the site of the earlier minster church, though no standing fabric in the building dates to before the 12th century.

The new community at Easby was probably originally 13 strong. It was drawn from Newhouse in Lincolnshire, the first Premonstratensian house in England, founded in about 1143. Easby almost immediately became involved in large-scale sheep farming. Over the course of the late 12th century it received further land bequests, including gifts from Conan, Duke of Brittany, who confirmed the foundation, and Richard de Rollos, who came into possession of part of the property attached to the constableship of the castle.

ACTIVITIES OF THE ABBOTS

The abbey's history is not well documented, but records of a number of legal cases shed some light on its affairs. There was a quarrel in 1284 over the abbey's use of a mill at Bolton-on-

Above: The cartulary of Easby, in which the records of the abbey were kept until its Dissolution in 1536

Below: Silver penny (top) of Henry III, 1216–72, and two medieval jettons (tokens used for calculations) found at Easby, one French and one German, depicting the lion of St Mark, with a small hole for suspension

Facing page: Photograph of visitors at Easby Abbey in the 1850s, by Joseph Cundall. The window visible is that in the south-west corner of the refectory

HISTORY OF EASBY: FURNISHINGS OF THE ABBEY

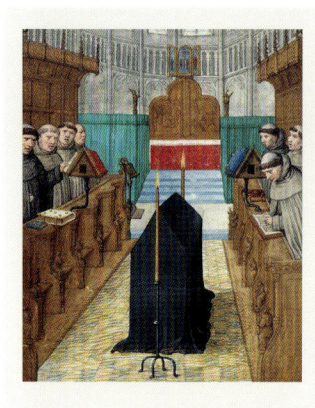

Above: Monks in their choir in the 16th century. The ornately carved stalls are similar to those from Easby, dating from about 1500 (detail of a Flemish manuscript of about 1516)

Right: The choir stalls from Easby Abbey, in the Church of St Mary, Richmond, as shown in a watercolour by William Callow in 1843, before their rearrangement as they appear today

Below: One of the medieval misericords from Easby Abbey, now in the choir of the Church of St Mary, Richmond

Furnishings of the Abbey

Remarkably, two early 16th-century furnishings from Easby were saved from destruction at the Dissolution

Church of St Mary, Richmond

The choir stalls from Easby Abbey are first documented in the parish church of Richmond in the 18th century, when they were botched together as pews. Later, in 1860, they were rearranged in their present form, as a choir, comprising two banks of seats, one to each side of the chancel, below a wooden canopy. The form of the canopy differs in detail from that of the original, though it incorporates the surviving medieval timber. Carved into it is an inscription, which includes sections of the early 16th-century original, listing breaches of monastic discipline: 'There are ten abuses of the cloister: a refined way of life, delicate food, gossip in the cloister, quarrelling in the chapter, discord in the choir, negligent pupils, disobedience of youth, stubbornness of age, obstinacy of the monks'.

When raised the stall seats reveal misericords (ledges upon which to lean when standing). Some of these are also

HISTORY OF EASBY: FURNISHINGS OF THE ABBEY

medieval. At the back of one choir canopy is carved the emblem of a barrel ('ton') overlaid with the letters 'ba', a visual pun on the name of Abbot Robert Bampton, the last Abbot of Easby, ruling from 1511 until the Dissolution. It was presumably he who commissioned the stalls for the choir of the abbey church.

Holy Trinity Church, Wensley

In the north aisle of the parish church of Wensley, close to the Scrope seat of Bolton Castle (see page 48), is a screen that originally stood in Easby Abbey. It was awkwardly reconfigured to form three sides of a family pew in the 17th century.

Originally, it had a single door (the present pew entrance was cut through it in the 17th century). The screen would have formed a division between the main body of the abbey church and one of its side chapels, evidently the resting place – presumably with grand associated tombs – of various members of the Scrope family of Bolton. Fragmentary inscribed sections of the screen, surviving in the cornice and on a rail of the pew, list various members of the Scrope family that 'here lyeth', including the 6th and 7th Barons Scrope of Bolton, both called Henry, and their wives, Elizabeth and Mabel. The 7th Baron died in 1533 and the screen was probably made soon afterwards.

The ornamentation of the screen includes family heraldry and complex tracery patterns of a type popular in northern England in the early 16th century. The colouring is modern, but the whole may originally have been painted.

In the chancel is a pair of medieval stall ends incorporated into the 19th-century stalls. They, too, are carved with Scrope family heraldry and may be related to the screen, suggesting that the abbey side chapel included seating for clergy. The screen and stalls were presumably rescued from Easby by the Scrope family at the Dissolution. Indeed, the then head of the family, John, the 8th Baron, had probably commissioned both the screen and its associated tombs for his father and grandfather.

Below: *The Scrope screen in Holy Trinity Church, Wensley. The arms on the screen celebrate the dynastic alliances of the Scrope family*

HISTORY OF EASBY: THE SCROPE PATRONAGE

Above: Many of the bequests made to Easby for the poor included instructions on what was to be given and when, as in John Romaine's list requesting red and white salted fish to be handed out on St Agatha's day; detail of a French manuscript showing a canon distributing fish to the needy

Below: The Scrope arms carved above the south door of the parish church of St Agatha. The Scropes of Bolton bought the patronage of Easby Abbey in 1333, and assumed the title of 'founders' of the abbey

Swale, about 2.5 miles downriver, which the servants of the abbot, John, stripped of iron in lieu of rent. In 1309 the then abbot, Roger, and six canons were accused of carrying off the possessions of the Abbot of St Mary's in York. Rather more intriguing is the resolution of a quarrel over an area of moorland in Barden about 4 miles away. The dispute had continued over the time of five abbots, but in 1311 Robert de Eglisclive conceded that he, his father and his grandfather had unjustly deprived the abbey of the land. Robert sought and was granted absolution by the abbot, but anxious for the souls of his ancestors, he asked that the abbot and his three surviving predecessors go to the tombs of his parents and grandfather, and pronounce absolution over them. This they did.

There are records of more usual affairs, such as a bequest made to the abbey in about 1250 by John Romaine, Archdeacon of Richmond, which laid out detailed requirements for the use of his gift. This included a weekly distribution to five poor people of 'as much meat and drink as came to 55s. 11d., a year', spending '26s. 8d. in giving one loaf of bread, one flagon of ale, and one mess of food, to one poor person every day, from the feast of All Souls to the feast of the Circumcision', and giving 'the value of £4 in corn and red and white salted fish, to every poor and indigent person on the day of St Agatha'.

THE SCROPE PATRONAGE

From before 1321 a descendant of the founder of the abbey, also called Roald, began to sell off his estates to Sir Geoffrey and Sir Henry Scrope (d.1336). The latter bought the patronage of Easby in 1333 and assumed the title of 'founder'. Henceforth the Scropes became patrons of the abbey and used the church as their dynastic mausoleum. Some sense of their family presence in the monastery is provided by the testimonies given in a celebrated legal case in 1385–90. It was brought against Sir Richard Grosvenor by Sir Henry's son, Richard Scrope (c.1327–1403), who by then had been made 1st Baron Scrope of Bolton (which castle he was building nearby) and had served as Chancellor of England. The disagreement was over the right to bear a coat-of-arms comprising a blue field with a gold sash (in heraldic terms, azure a bend or).

The Abbot of Easby testified in 1386 that the tomb of the father of Richard 'lies in the said abbey under the chancel … [his] effigy graven in stone, and painted with the said arms … and several others of his lineage are buried … under flat stones, and above the same stones graven flatly their images in sculpture, and their shields portrayed by sculpture, on which are their arms; and by the side of the shield is pictured a naked sword; and their arms in glass all over the church of St Agatha, in windows, in tablets before altars, in the vestments of the said abbey, in chambers, in the glass of the chambers, in the glass of the windows of the refectory'.

HISTORY OF EASBY: PILGRIMAGE OF GRACE

In 1392 Richard Scrope acquired a licence to endow the abbey with lands worth £150 per annum for the support of a further 10 chaplains, 2 priests and 22 poor men at the abbey. His will of 1400 also gifted the abbot as an heirloom a cup and cover given to him by Edward, the Black Prince.

This close relationship between the abbey and the Scrope family continued until the eve of the Reformation. In 1534, after the death of his father, John, 8th Baron Scrope of Bolton, was welcomed at the abbey 'as our veray trewe and undoubted founder of our said monasterye, with procession and such other solempnities and ceremonises as doth perteyne and belong thereunto, according as our predecessors have heretofore at all times received his noble ancestours as founders of the sayme'.

The document goes on to promise that John and his heirs will be 'partakers of all out praers, suffragies, and other devoute and meritorious actes and good deids, but also all other customes, dueties, pleasors and comodites, whiche dothe apperteyne and belonge unto the just title and right of a founder'. It was probably John who commissioned the furniture for the Scrope family chapel (see page 47).

PILGRIMAGE OF GRACE

In 1535 Henry VIII ordered the valuation of the properties of the Church. In early 1536 two agents for the king, Richard Layton and Thomas Legh, visited Easby and reported that it had an annual income, once all charges, pensions and other expenses were paid, of £111 17s. It consequently fell victim to

Above: The stall plate of John (1437–98), 5th Baron Scrope of Bolton, as a Knight of the Garter, at St George's Chapel, Windsor

Below left: An embroidered banner of the Five Wounds of Christ carried by one Thomas Constable on the Pilgrimage of Grace in 1536, a popular uprising against the king's Suppression of the Monasteries

Below: An abbot's crozier thought to have been in use at Easby Abbey; it came originally from France and dates from 1150 to 1175

HISTORY OF EASBY: AFTER THE DISSOLUTION

Above: An impression of the seal of Easby Abbey. When the abbey was suppressed, the Duke of Norfolk, who had been sent to enforce the closure, sent the seal to London as a sign that his work was done

Below: Easby Abbey from the south-west in about 1670, by Francis Place. By this time the abbey was leased to the Scrope family and the abbey buildings were already partly in ruin, as can be seen below

the dissolution of the lesser monastic houses ordered in 1535. Layton and Legh also claimed that five canons were guilty of sodomy, one was incontinent (lacking in sexual self-restraint) and two desired release from their vows. Abbot Robert and his community of 17 canons surrendered their property to the Crown. The abbot was given a pension of 40 marks.

Across England there was deep popular resentment at the closure of the monasteries. Stirred by this and other grievances, the populace of Richmond joined in the Pilgrimage of Grace in 1536, the largest popular uprising of Henry VIII's reign. The agent of the Dissolution Richard Layton was one of those the pilgrimage called to be punished. After persuading the 'pilgrims' to disperse, Henry VIII revenged himself upon the entire region, raising his banner in sign of open war upon his own subjects. Writing on 22 February 1537 to the Duke of Norfolk, the commander of his forces in the north, the king instructed: 'you must cause such dreadful execution upon a good number of the inhabitants, hanging them on trees, quartering them and setting their heads and quarters in every town as shall be a fearful warning … [and] as these troubles have been promoted by the monks and canons of these parts, at your repair to Salley, Hexham, Newminster, Lanercost, St Agatha and other places as have made resistance … you shall without pity or circumstance, now that our banner is displayed, cause the monks to be tied up without further delay.' It is not known what actually befell Easby Abbey or the local population, at this instruction, but the Duke of Norfolk sent the seal of the abbey to London on 28 June 1537.

AFTER THE DISSOLUTION

After the Dissolution a parcel of the abbey's former property, including Easby, was leased to the Scrope family. In the early 18th century they broke up the land and sold it off, Easby passing to the rector of neighbouring Melsonby, Reverend William Smith. He built the manor house overlooking the ruins. Further important changes to the buildings were probably undertaken by one Robert Jaques, who in turn bought the property in 1816 for £45,000.

Visitations to the Abbey

A visitation was a formal enquiry into the state of a community and its findings were recorded.

The most fully documented years of the abbey are 1478 to 1500, when the Principal of the English Premonstratensian Province, Bishop Richard Redman (d.1505; see page 39), regularly came to Easby on visitation. At his visit of 1482, for example, it was recorded that a certain John Nym was fugitive from the community and was to be judged by a tribunal for his faults. Nym was accused of incontinence (lack of sexual self-restraint) with a widow, Elizabeth Wales. He was subsequently found innocent of the charge and by 1494 had risen to be prior (the deputy of the abbot) of the abbey. In his 1482 visit Redman directed the abbot to allow access to the warming room or calefactory before and after meals when the weather was cold; the prior to make sure that the brethren did not make dissolute conversation; that no one got to bed without a tunic, hose and girdle on pain of a day's bread and water; and that silence be properly observed. He went on to say that the community was in debt and concluded by praising the overall state of the monastery, which was well provided with food and new buildings. This reference to buildings may be to the extensive 15th-century alterations to the abbey.

In other years Redman commented on the practice of devotion in the church, educating the novices, the treatment of the sick, absence from the monastic enclosure and drinking after Compline (the last office of the evening). There also survive lists of the community over this period, which evidently fluctuated in size between 15 and 24, including priests and novices.

Above: *The tomb of Bishop Richard Redman in Ely Cathedral*

Below: *During his tenure as Principal of the English Premonstratensian Province, from 1478 to 1500, Bishop Redman regularly visited Easby to check on the state of the community and offer instruction. In this English manuscript of 1487 a visiting bishop blesses a kneeling cleric*

HISTORY OF EASBY: AFTER THE DISSOLUTION

Above: A view of Easby Abbey, with Richmond Castle and town in the distance and the 18th-century manor house on the right, by George Cuitt in about 1800, when both castle and abbey were popular romantic ruins

Below right: The refectory of Easby Abbey from the parish churchyard

A description of the abbey published by William Clarkson in 1821 speaks of the improvements made 'by altering the road, opening many beautiful doorways and windows which had been walled up and throwing down some useless modern walls that confined and crowded too much upon the abbey'. Easby had been transformed into a romantic ruin. Robert Jaques lived to the ripe age of 75 and his monument can be seen in Easby church.

In 1886 the Council of the Yorkshire Archaeological Society made funds available for the eminent monastic historian William St John Hope to excavate the site. He revealed the full layout of the monastery and published a history of the site. In February 1926 an article in the *Yorkshire Post* complained of the state of the abbey and called for the Office of Works to take it in charge. When they did so in the 1930s the ruins were stripped back to their medieval core. The abbey is now in the care of the English Heritage Trust.